D0683734

# LECTIO DIVINA

Mario Masini

# Lectio Divina

## An Ancient Prayer
## That Is Ever New

Translated by Edmund C. Lane, SSP

ALBA · HOUSE      NEW · YORK

SOCIETY OF ST. PAUL, 2187 VICTORY BLVD., STATEN ISLAND, NEW YORK 10314

**ST PAULS**

Originally published in Italian by Edizioni San Paolo, s.r.l.,
under the title *Lectio Divina: Preghiera Antica e Nuova*.

Library of Congress Cataloging-in-Publication Data

Masini, Mario, 1927-
    [Lectio divina. English]
    Lectio divina: an ancient prayer that is ever new / Mario
  Masini; translated by Edmund C. Lane.
      p.    cm.
  Includes bibliographical references.
  ISBN 0-8189-0813-0
  1. Prayer — Catholic Church. 2. Spiritual life — Catholic
Church. 3. Bible — Devotional use.  I. Title.
BX2350.65.M334     1998
248.3 — dc21                     97-48930
                                     CIP

Produced and designed in the United States of America by the
Fathers and Brothers of the Society of St. Paul,
2187 Victory Boulevard, Staten Island, New York 10314,
as part of their communications apostolate.

ISBN: 0-8189-0813-0

**Printing Information:**

Current Printing - first digit      2  3  4  5  6  7  8  9  10

Year of Current Printing - first year shown

          2000   2001   2002   2003   2004   2005

# Table of Contents

# Introduction

The rediscovery of *lectio divina* runs parallel to a return to the study of the Bible on the part of the Christian faithful. Both follow the recommendations of the Second Vatican Council as set forth in the magisterial documents of the contemporary Church in a crescendo which witnesses to the widespread attention now being given to *lectio divina*. Four recent documents go out of their way to mention it:

1. The *Catechism of the Catholic Church* (1992): "The *lectio divina*, where the Word of God is so read and meditated that it becomes prayer, is thus rooted in the liturgical celebration" (1177).

2. *The Interpretation of the Bible in the Church* of the Pontifical Biblical Commission (1993): "*Lectio divina* is a reading, on an individual or communal level, of a more or less lengthy passage of Scripture, received as the Word of God and leading, at the prompting of the Spirit, to meditation, prayer and contemplation." "Insis-

tence on *lectio divina* in both its forms, individual and communal, has therefore become a reality once more." "Many initiatives for communal reading have been launched among Christians and one can only encourage this desire to derive from Scripture a better knowledge of God and of his plan of salvation in Jesus Christ" (IV, C, 2).

3. *Pastoral Note of the Italian Episcopal Conference* (1995): "*Lectio divina*, present in the tradition of the Church from ancient times, is a theologically solid and secure spiritual experience, pedagogically accessible to all and highly efficacious in the maturation of one's faith." "Originally practiced in monastic circles, today *lectio divina* is becoming ever more available to all the faithful in Christ and represents a true grace of God with which to initiate every Christian into a life of prayer." "The practice of *lectio divina* should be introduced and continuously sustained by a reflection which sets forth the reason behind it and explains well its identity, its objectives and its methods." "The very powerful evangelical transformation that accompanies it should be stressed" (31).

4. *Consecrated Life* (Vita Consecrata), *Post-Synodal Exhortation of the Holy Father, Pope John Paul II* (1996): Thanks to *lectio divina*, "the word of God is brought to bear on life, on which it

projects that light of wisdom which is a gift of the Spirit.... Indeed it would be helpful if this practice were also encouraged among other members of the People of God, priests and laity alike" (94).

The text offered here responds not only to these invitations, but also to the presentation of the "meaning" and the "steps" involved in the practice of *lectio divina*: listening to and interpreting the biblical text (=*lectio*), deepening and taking to oneself its message (=*meditatio*), sharing it with others (=*collatio*), transforming the word of God into prayer (=*oratio* and *contemplatio*), and finally witnessing to the word as a committed Christian (=*operatio*).

# LECTIO DIVINA

# *"Lectio divina"*

For some years now the expression "*lectio divina*" has become more or less commonplace, but the ways in which it is understood are far from being the same. For some, in fact, *lectio divina* refers to any meditation or reflection whatsoever which has some relationship to the Bible. It is necessary, therefore, to define first of all what *lectio divina* really is and to show that it always ends in prayer.

## 1. The expression *"lectio divina"*

An initial understanding of *lectio divina* comes from a consideration of the words themselves.

### 1.1. The noun *"lectio"*

The term *lectio* (=reading) refers to the act of reading, but derives etymologically from the Latin verb "*lego,*" which includes the concept of "tying together," "gathering up," "harvesting." In reference to *lectio* the last of these terms brings to mind that, along with being a simple, albeit intelligent and accurate "reading" of a biblical text, *lectio* looks to "glean" or "harvest" the message which is expressed by it. For that reason Guerric of Igny (12th century) exhorted: "You who hastily peruse the garden of Scripture, imitate the industrious bee who collects from all the flowers the honey it produces."

*Lectio divina* is not a "study" undertaken for scientific purposes. Nevertheless the respect and veneration due the word of God require the avoidance, in interpreting it, of any careless, slipshod, or slovenly approach which might lead to "a dangerous slip into a kind of distorted biblicism" (*Pastoral Note of the Italian Episcopal Conference*, 11). To this end the acquisition of some exegetical expertise will come in handy.

The Cistercian abbot, Isaac of Stella (12th century) teaches the need to bring together two fundamental approaches to the goal of an authentic *lectio divina.* Making good use of the typology of St. Luke about welcoming Jesus (10:38-42), he advises us to "keep the solicitude of Martha without losing the devotion of Mary." The "solicitude of Martha" is emblematic of the hard work needed to have a correct understanding of the written word of God; the "devotion of Mary" expresses the warmth and loving openness to what the word says to its reader-listener. The same lesson can be rephrased using an expression full of biblical pathos by referring to the two "trees" of the "garden of Eden" (Gn 2:9): Maintain "the link between the tree of knowledge and the tree of life" (G.-M. Oury), for, in fact, "knowledge" contributes to "life."

Practiced in this fashion, *lectio divina* brings to the soul "the message of God's love which seeks me out," according to the expression of St. Bernard (12th century), and provides a way to establish a heart-to-heart contact with God.

## 1.2. The adjective "*divina*"

In traditional Christian language, the modifier "*divina*" intends to convey first of all the idea that in *lectio divina* there takes place, through the holy page, the *sacra pagina*, an encounter of man with the word of God, with "the divine Word of truth and wisdom," an encounter that "inflames and illumines more than the power of the sun" and that reaches "the depths of the heart and mind" (St. Justin, 2nd century) of the one at prayer.

The adjective "*divina*" moreover seeks to signify the search, through Scripture, for an encounter with God by means of the Holy Spirit, who — always, but in a particular way in *lectio divina* — "opens the mind to an understanding of the Scriptures" (cf. Lk 24:45), and who "leads us to the whole truth" (Jn 16:13), "teaching us all things" and "causing us to recall all that Jesus has taught" (Jn 14:26). In fact, "whoever holds that he can unlock the secrets of Scripture without the Spirit of God, will lose his way like a person who seeks a goal in the dark, groping along unfamiliar walls" (Guibert, 11th century). In *lectio divina* the divine word is luminous because "under the effect of the revealing action of the Spirit our spirit expands and is raised to a level where it can understand the Scriptures" (Henry of Marcy, 12th century).

"*Lectio*" and "*divina*" are two terms which, when joined, indicate that in the Bible God speaks through the enlightenment of the Spirit.

## 2. The Word, the Book, the Expression

Recalling certain theological facts will contribute to our illustration of the meaning, which we have just synthesized, of *lectio divina* and at the same time it will open up new horizons to us.

Above all: the Bible is the book of the word of God. But which word is present in this book?

## 2.1. The Word, the word of God

This is taught us by a passage — with high theological content — from the Gospel of John (1:1): "The Word was God." This affirmation attests to the reality of the Word of God and expresses a fundamental certainty of *lectio divina.* The evangelist did not write that the Word was "divine," that is, that it belonged to the sphere of divinity. He stated instead that the Word *is* God, that is, it is the Second Person of the Divine Trinity.

This affirmation teaches us something very important. *Lectio divina* banishes any attempt to make the word of God equal to the Word of God: the Word of God is not present in Scripture with the same realism that Christ is present sacramentally in the Eucharist. But it also banishes a complete separation between Scripture and the Word of God, as if in Scripture there were only his message. The Bible is the word of God because there is present in it, in a certain measure, the same Word/word of the Father. The liturgy today is expressed with the same realism that it had in the 10th century: "In the Gospel, Christ speaks from his own lips to his people."

*Lectio divina* approaches the Bible in the knowledge of being able to truly enter, by means of the word, into contact with the Word of God. To hold that the Bible is only a message greatly impoverishes its reality. Instead, *lectio divina* knows that Scripture renders possible an ineffable encounter with the Word of God in the reality of his divinity. This "encounter" is the highly exalted and very ambitious goal towards which *lectio divina* proceeds, with joy and fatigue, on its pilgrimage.

## 2.2. The Word became flesh

John also sketches a history of the Word, condensing it in two expressions: the Word "became flesh" and "dwelt among us" (Jn 1:14). Thus begins the story of the Word in the history of mankind: without ceasing to be that which He is in the mystery of the Trinity, the Word takes up a journey which theology will formalize with the term "Incarnation."

The truth of the Incarnation is far from being extraneous to *lectio divina*. Not only because in the Incarnation the eternal Word becomes the One who is the truth of all the Scriptures. But also because the Incarnation constitutes the historical-theological foundation for which "the Word become flesh" is also "the Word become book."

## 2.3. The Word became book

The realism of the Incarnation was also used by the ancient Fathers of the Church as an objective reference to explain the way in which the Word of God can be present in Scripture. Already in the 3rd century, Origen reflected on the words "to become flesh," on the assumption of visible and tangible concreteness on the part of the divine Word. He recognized two ways in which this took place: in the Incarnation the Word "became Jesus"; in Scripture, the Word "became book." Granted that there remains a substantial and very real difference, it must be seen that in the Incarnation as in Scripture, there is a real presence, albeit mysterious, of the Word of God.

To show the dual mode of presence of the Word here we will use the expressions "incarnation" (=Word made flesh), and "inverbation" (=Word made book). Christians encounter the Word of God in the "Word made flesh" and also in the "Word made book": to the two modes of presence of the Word of God corresponds two possibilities of encountering Him. *Lectio divina* seeks Him above all in his "inverbation."

*Lectio divina* lives the knowledge which God continues to utter, or rather that God continues to communicate of himself, so that, even in the text of Scripture the Word/word of God is present. The Bible is the place *in which* God has fixed his word, and it is also the place *from which* He speaks even in our day and age.

## 3. The Spirit and the Word

The work of the Holy Spirit with respect to Scripture and its *lectio* has to do, not with a hazy and vaguely mystical concept, but with a truth founded on a theology that is both solid and spiritually enriching.

### 3.1. From the Spirit, the Word

"All Scripture is inspired by God" (2 Tm 3:16). This New Testament affirmation declares the relationship between Scripture, God and the Holy Spirit of God. This was stated explicitly by the Second Vatican Council (Dogmatic Constitution on Divine Revelation, *Dei Verbum*, 11) in this fashion: "The divinely revealed realities, which are contained and presented in the text of Sacred Scripture, have been written down under the inspiration of the Holy Spirit," in this way synthesizing what had been taught uninterruptedly by the Fathers of the Church. One of these, St.

Ambrose (4th century), expressed the role of the Spirit this way: "God inspired what the Holy Spirit says in Scripture." Therefore, in Sacred Scripture the Holy Spirit speaks the Word of God.

These affirmations make up the fundamental teaching behind the *lectio divina*: the Bible, while made up of a written text, in reality is "Word." It is the Word *par excellence* which is the "Word of God" (Jn 1:1) concretized, in a certain way, in the Bible. This is made possible through the working of the Holy Spirit: to Him is equally owed the incarnation of the Word in the womb of the Virgin as well as the inverbation of the Word in Scripture.

For this reason *lectio divina* considers the written text of the Bible as but a "cloud": beyond it shines the "sun" of the living Word (Alan of Lille, 12th century). It is guided by this certainty that *lectio divina* approaches the Scriptures.

## 3.2. The Spirit of the Word

The Spirit not only "inspires," but "inhabits" Scripture. And He "inhabits" it as "a light which causes the grace of God's Light to be set free" (St. Gregory of Nyssa, 4th century). The presence of the Holy Spirit in the Word finds its fulfillment when the Christian arrives at the truth of Scripture, of God and of Christ.

Even the early Fathers, who had frequent contact with the Scriptures, often experienced them as "a closed writing," a "sealed book" (Simeon the New Theologian, 11th century), which "hid profound and arcane meanings" (Gottfried of Admont, 12th century). Above all, the Scriptures resembled an "immense sea of secrets which we are obliged to confront with the fragile barks of our intelligence."

Our intelligence with its innate capabilities alone is not able to breach the barriers beyond which the secrets of the Divine Word shine and arrive at the port of illumination. It can, however, succeed in doing so with the help of the Holy Spirit, who, according to Origen, is the "exegete of Scripture." He, in fact, "unlocks (the coffers), manifests and renders visible and comprehensible things hidden and closed," "unseals the 'book,' and gives the reader the sense of Scripture" (Simeon the New Theologian). And so "if God gives (to the 'fragile bark' of our intelligence) the 'wind' favorable to the 'Spirit,' we will be able to arrive at the port of a profound comprehension of the Scriptures" (Origen).

"Things pertaining to God and to our salvation cannot be understood without the Holy Spirit," and so "no one can presume to be able to penetrate in depth divine secrets and the Scriptures with his own wisdom alone. Never is an exact interpretation of Scripture given without the teaching and guidance of the Holy Spirit" (Richard of Saint-Victor, 12th century). "As our eyes do not see without light, our ears do not hear without sound, so the human soul cannot know the things of God if the light of the Holy Spirit is not given to it" (St. Hilary of Poitiers, 4th century). The Spirit gives us "a knowledge of the mysteries and provides us with a familiarity with the things of heaven as well" (St. Basil, 4th century).

*Lectio divina* lives off the knowledge that every light given for the understanding of Scripture and of the mysteries of God comes as a gift from the Holy Spirit.


## 3.3. From the Word, the Spirit

In reference to the Spirit, the Scriptures stand in passive expectation in so far as they are inspired and illuminated by Him. But they also stand in active expectation because from them the Holy Spirit communicates Himself.

This has been explained well by Origen. In his vision, the Holy Spirit exercises a triple role, expressed by him with the penetrating insight of the consummate interpreter of the Bible, through the skillful use of the variations in the prefix of the Greek verb "to breathe" (*spirare* in Latin): "The sacred books 'breathe again' (*re-spirare*) the 'fullness' of the Holy Spirit. As a consequence, even today they 'breathe forth' (*ex-spirare*) the words of that 'fullness.' And those who have eyes are 'inspired' (*in-spirare*) because they see heavenly things, those who have ears because they hear divine mysteries, those who have noses because they perceive the reality of that 'fullness'." That which the Holy Spirit "breathes forth" (*ex-spirare*) and which "inspires" (*in-spirare*) those who read the Scriptures is specified by Origen in one word: "Wisdom. And there is not a word of Holy Scripture that is deprived of the wisdom of God."

To the practitioner of *lectio divina* who prayerfully asks that "the Spirit of wisdom be present" (St. Gregory the Great, 6th century), the Spirit grants wisdom. According to the mystical vision of the Eastern Church, the Holy Spirit is "God's theologian" and at the same time "the Christian's inner teacher." Thus whoever knows how to be "receptive to the Holy Spirit" acquires (according to Macarius the Egyptian, 4th century), the "knowledge of God," that is, wisdom.

## 3.4. The Word of Wisdom

According to the New Testament, "the wisdom of God" is "Christ Jesus" (1 Cor 1:24, 2:2). Bestowing wisdom, the Holy Spirit therefore leads us above all to recognize Christ in the Scriptures. In fact "all of Sacred Scripture — the Old as well as the New Testament — points to Christ" (Gottfried of Admont). The first level of Christian wisdom consists in the recognition of the "Christ-significance" of all of Scripture, because "the goal of the Scriptures is Christ" (Luther).

Wisdom also leads to another level: that of giving to the reader of Scripture "the mind" of Christ (1 Cor 2:16) rendering the reader capable of sharing "the very attitude of Christ" (Ph 2:5) and even "the concerns of the Spirit" (Rm 8:6). There exists, in fact, a reciprocity between Christ and the Spirit: "Christ gives to man the Spirit; the Spirit communicates to man the spirit of Christ" (L. Cerfaux).

Wisdom, then, is the capacity to understand the Scriptures "spiritually," that is to recognize Christ in them in the entirety of His mystery-truth by means of the light and under the guidance of the Holy Spirit. The *lectio* of the Scriptures is a privileged way to acquire that most exalted wisdom which is "Christ, in whom are hidden all the treasures of wisdom and knowledge" (Col 2:3).

To prevent any unwarranted illusions, Evagrius Ponticus (4th century) defines the role of Scripture in the acquisition of wisdom: "To expect to be taught directly by the Holy Spirit without meditation on the word of God is a false hope." Instead, it is through the Scriptures read in the light and understood in the grace of the Spirit that *lectio divina* enters into the profound mystery and full truth of God in Christ.

## 4. To Christ through the Spirit

Jesus said that after His ascension, He would send from heaven the Holy Spirit who would introduce believers "into the whole truth" (Jn 16:13). In the thought of the Fourth Evangelist the "truth" is Christ in the reality of His person. He would guide us to the truth, "the whole truth," and lead us into the "mystery of Christ" in all His fullness, the "breadth and length, height and depth" of Him and of His "inscrutable riches" (Eph 3:18, 8), that is to the entirety of the reality of Christ.

## 4.1. Through the Spirit, the "mind" of Christ

According to St. Paul there exists a category of Christians whom he calls "spiritual," that is, persons transformed and animated by the "Spirit" of the Son "sent by God into their hearts" (cf. Gal 4:6). Through the presence of the Spirit these individuals are rich in the "mind of Christ" (1 Cor 2:15-16).

The word "mind" designates (among other things) the possibility Christians have of acquiring a "mentality" by means of which they see, think, judge, and choose with the very "mind" of Christ himself. The "mind of Christ" is the greatest of the "gifts of God" (cf. 1 Cor 2:12) with which the Holy Spirit enriches man: by means of such a gift Christians are configured to Christ and thus come to their own authentic truth.

"Spiritual" persons are those who share the "attitude of Christ" (Ph 2:5), or, to put it another way, who make the "concerns of the Spirit" (Rm 8:6) their own. The Spirit enables Christians to enter into the mystery of Christ, manifesting Him to them and sharing Him with them. And so Christians are able, in the Spirit, to know Christ "according to the Spirit," that is, they are able to know the truth of the Word Incarnate and Risen Lord, and to live lives in conformity to the reality of the Incarnate, Glorified Lord. This is what Paul wants to convey when he writes: "We possess the 'mind' of Christ."

*Lectio divina* is a means — and not an inconsiderable one — at the disposition of the Spirit to give to those who practice it the "mind of Christ." Orthodox theology expresses this possibility through the use of two characteristic terms: "The Spirit-bearing (that is, those enriched with the Holy Spirit) become Christ-bearing (that is, those enriched with Christ)" (P. Evdokimov).

## 4.2. Christ, Truth of the Scriptures

*Lectio divina* uses the text of Scripture but it hopes to arrive at a much higher, more "substantial" objective: an encounter with "Christ according to the Spirit" (Rm 1:4).

Christ is at the same time the Word which speaks in the Bible and the Word of which the Bible speaks. He not only brings the truth, but *is* the Truth: "He is at one and the same time the messenger and the content of the message, the Revealer and the revealed: the Revealer whom we must believe, and the personal Truth revealed *in which* we must believe" (H. de Lubac). Christ is "revealed" not only in His words, but also in His actions and in His very Person. When it manages to "discover" Christ in the plenitude of His truth, to "encounter" Christ in the fullness of His mystery, *lectio divina* has crossed the threshold of the "written Word" and entered into communion with the "substantial Word," with "Christ according to the Spirit."

This is true of the *lectio* of the New Testament texts because "Christ is the Gospel" (Amalarius of Metz, 9th century). But it is also true of the Old Testament writings: in fact even "the Old Testament points to Christ" (Gottfried of Admont). But Christ is also more than the goal, the truth, the fulfillment of Scripture; He is also its "spirit" (St. Bernard).

Seeking and finding Christ in Scripture, those who practice *lectio divina* arrive at the "spiritual sense given by the Spirit" (Origen), and ascend to the "peak of their spiritual intelligence" (Jerome); "they have reached the summit and there remains nothing more for them to discover." Following this, "by the grace of God, as they grow ever more in the light, so shall they increase ever more in love" (Cassiodorus, 5th century).

## 4.3. Christ, the Word "abbreviated"

The Fathers of the early Church revealed that, in Old Testament times, a multiplicity of divine words could be heard: "God had pronounced only one Word (His own Word), but many words were heard" (Ambrose). Such a multiplicity allowed "the expansion of the one Word of God into the whole of Scripture" (Augustine), and still its readers never did succeed in recognizing the bright thread that tied all of them together into one.

Using the same expressions of the Fathers, H. de Lubac synthesized their teaching in this way: Jesus is "the Word 'abbreviated,' 'concentrated,' in the sense that the contents of the whole of Scripture is unified, fulfilled, illuminated and transcended in Him." Hence "the Book is Christ" (Absalon, 12th century).

United to the conviction regarding a certain presence of the Word of God Himself in Scripture (which we have already considered), recognition of the concentration of Scripture in Christ is fundamental to every interpretation of the Bible and constitutes the correct methodology for the practice of *lectio divina.* Peter Cantor (12th century) expressed the relationship between Scripture and the Word Incarnate in this way: "Twice the Father 'abbreviated' His Word: in the Word on the holy page and in the tiny womb of the Virgin." According to the Christian vision, the history of the Old Testament represents a long climb to reach the summit. This summit is Christ. The multiplicity of words and events in the Old Testament are 'abbreviated' in Christ insofar as "all of Scripture speaks of Him and finds in Him its truth" (Hugh of Saint-Victor, 12th century).

The Gospel, too, can be called an "abbreviated word" (Jerome), or even "a most abbreviated word" (Guerric of Igny), because it brings everything together in one person: Jesus. "We heard the 'abbreviated word' (the Gospel) of the 'Word abbreviated' (Jesus)" (Garnerius of Rochefort, 13th century). Jesus is "the Word who 'abbreviates' and brings all to completion in holiness. Word of love, Word of every perfection" (Aelred of Rievaulx, 12th century).

"The many words pronounced by God are, then, but one Word: *the* Word" (Rupert of Deutz, 11th century). There follows a grave warning and a powerful invitation to those who practice *lectio divina.* The warning: whoever reads Scripture "without discovering Christ the Wisdom of God there," contained in it in its very letter, "is a fool who has understood nothing of Scripture" (Erveus of Bourg-Dieu, 12th century). The invitation is this: to strive to discover in Scripture "Christ, the basis of all truth" and then "to comprehend its mystery: Christ" (Gottfried of Admont).

## 5. The dimensions of "*lectio divina*"

Christians have always hailed the great effort of exegetes to identify interpretive "keys" which might guide them in their understanding of the Word of God.

The utility of such "keys" was illustrated by Origen in the famous parable of the "house with many locked rooms. Next to each room a key was placed, which however did not correspond to the one which would open that door." It was necessary therefore to find the proper "key" to open the various and diverse "rooms" inhabited by the divine Word.

The "keys" identified by hermeneutics are many: we recall only those which come from antiquity, because in these are implicit also those discovered in modern times. These open up the "sense," that is, the significance of the biblical text. These are explained by St. Thomas Aquinas (13th century) in this highly lucid synthesis: "Let us consider the expression: 'Let there be light' (cf. Gn 1:3). If by 'light' physical light is intended, we have the *literal sense*. If by 'light' we refer to the light of Christ, we are dealing with the *allegorical or symbolic sense*. If we say 'light' intending that our intelligence is enlightened and our heart drawn by Christ, we are expressing the *tropological or morally edifying sense.* If we use 'light' to signify that Christ will introduce us into glory, we are using the *anagogical or mystical sense."*

## 5.1. Literal Interpretation: the "literal sense"

The first and most fundamental significance of the Bible lies in its "literal sense," that which results from a determination of the meaning of the text. Insofar as it is expressed directly by the inspired human author it is the sense willed even by God who is the principal author of the Bible.

St. Augustine taught: "This is the rule: persist in a consideration of the 'letter.'" In fact, "the explanation of the 'letter' constitutes that which is fundamental" (Origen), which "must be established before anything else" (Gregory the Great), because "only amateurs do not give importance (in building) to the foundation" (Augustine).

Even for *lectio divina* the first duty consists in obtaining a "grasp of the 'letter'" (Origen). "A spiritual comprehension of the Scriptures is that much more solid the more it is firmly based on the literal sense" (Richard of Saint-Victor). In fact, in order that it be due to the inspiration of the Holy Spirit, "the literal sense is already, at least initially, the spiritual sense" (I. de la Potterie).

The "time" of *lectio divina* called "*lectio*" is

dedicated precisely to a listening to the biblical text in its literal sense.

The Fathers taught the need, however, of not getting bogged down in the "open plains of the narrative"; the meaning of Scripture is captured when it is understood in its "spirit" through the guidance of the "Spirit." St. Gregory the Great proclaimed this in the aphorism: "With one and the same word the Bible expounds the text and enunciates a mystery." In the divine word there are, therefore, two levels present at the same time: that which is said and that which is announced, what *is* and what *will be*, the "text" and the "mystery" which is in the text and goes beyond the text.

St. Ambrose has left us a commendable expression worthy of profound reflection on the part of both those who interpret Scripture as well as on the part of those who practice *lectio divina*: "The Word increases or diminishes according to the capacity" that each one has for discovering it and recognizing it. For the purpose of recognizing and gleaning the fullness of the Word in Sacred Scripture the Fathers have come up with and used interpretive "keys" which aim at discovering the depth and scope of the teaching which have the "letter" as their point of departure. We will come back to this a little further on.

## 5.2. Symbolical Interpretation:
### the "allegorical sense"

The "allegorical sense" consists in the transposition of some biblical texts from their obvious meaning to another, not evident in itself but evident to faith, which is able to recognize it because "faith certainly has eyes" (Augustine). Father M.-D. Chenu teaches that the "allegorical sense" gets its power from the allusive value of a biblical text in order to make it serve the "edification of faith," that is, in order to give it a broader and more diverse understanding than what is already believed. The allegorical sense restates the "content" of the faith, present in a general way in the Scriptures, for the purpose of the "edification of the reader-listener in the faith," that is for the purpose of keeping the reader-listener in the certainty of his belief while leading him toward an increasing enlightenment.

Allegorical interpretation is exposed to the risk — and this is its shortcoming — of putting too much distance between itself and the "letter" of the text, thus reaching conclusions which are too facile or even fantastic. All the same it presents an undoubted utility in the field of spirituality and pastoral practice, above all in preaching and in the understanding of liturgical language.

The "allegorical sense" offers itself as one way of approaching a fuller understanding of Scripture. It responds to one of the natural goals of *lectio divina*, which seeks to nourish one's faith. The allegorical sense contributes to this end by teaching us to read the Scriptures "with the eyes of the soul" (Origen), "with the eyes of the heart" (Jerome), "with our inner eye" (Augustine).

## 5.3. Morally Edifying Interpretation: the "tropological sense"

Scripture is read in the "tropological sense" when we search in it for teachings regarding how we ought to act. For example, about prayer Jesus taught us: "When you pray, go to your room and close the door; pray to your Father in secret" (Mt 6:6). Jesus explained the literal sense in these words: "When you pray, do not act like the hypocrites who love to pray standing in the synagogues and on street corners so that others may see them" (Mt 6:5). Jesus invites us to avoid exterior acts which smell of religious exhibitionism and, instead, to look for secluded places which favor our encounter with the Father "in secret." And thus the word "room" can be understood in a metaphorical sense, expressive of this "secluded place" fit for prayer.

St. Ambrose keeps the literal meaning of the word "room" and at the same time extends it in an allegorical-tropological sense, explaining: "Intend not a 'room' defined by the walls where your person is closed in, but the 'cell' which is within you, where your thoughts are enclosed and your sentiments make themselves felt." Note the progressive deepening of his understanding of the word: the "room" becomes the "cell"; the "cell" is still a "room," but it is the silent and solitary room of a monk; in its turn, the "cell" is changed into that most personal of secret places which every person of prayer has within himself and in which he is able to establish a dialogue with God and enter into a communion with Him marked by interiority.

The "tropological sense" has nothing, therefore, in common with a moralistic reading of the Bible. It responds to a very definite end: to extract from the sacred text teachings which are helpful in one's growth in love or charity, which is the summary of the Christian life.

5.4. Mystical Interpretation:
   the "anagogical sense"

The "anagogical sense" refers to an interpretation which looks "from afar," at eschatological realities, and which tends toward things "on high," toward realities superior to those of the Christian life, those belonging to "the hope which awaits us in heaven" (Col 1:5).

The "anagogical sense" refers to the last things — those which are to come — with Jesus as exemplar. He, in fact, is "the dawn in chiaroscuro" (Bernard); his "resurrection is both cause and model" (Guerric of Igny), because "Christ risen from the dead is the firstfruits of those who have fallen asleep" (1 Cor 15:20).

The interpretation of Scripture in an "anagogical sense" teaches us to relate the signs and truths of these ultimate realities to penultimate realities — those of today, and to make the "'eternal Gospel' (Rv 14:6), that which will be revealed when all shadows have passed and the truth has appeared, when death will have been destroyed and immortality begun" (Origen), understood now and for now.

The "anagogical sense" also has a specific goal: to help the reader to "grow in hope." *Lectio divina* patiently scrutinizes the literal sense in order to discover in it "realities which are eternal, spiritual, celestial," and thus "true" (St. Irenaeus, 2nd century). In fact, "Providence has arranged everything like a ladder that we must climb" to the eternal (Augustine), so that "we might pass from carnality to spirituality, from temporality to eternity" (St. Gregory Nazianzen, 4th century).

The "senses" we have recalled have been imagined by the Fathers as ways which give access to the profound meaning of the Scriptures while at the same time acting as steps to be climbed to an ever greater comprehension of them. They prove useful to the practice of *lectio divina*: the "literal" to *lectio*, the "allegorical" and "anagogical" to *meditatio* (meditation), and the "tropological" opens the way to action (*operatio*).

## 6. *Lectio divina* for the *Verbum divinum*

*Lectio divina* is an experience and as such is difficult to capture within the limitations of a definition. For that reason it allows for the manifestation, albeit essentially always and only partially, of its meaning through expressions which are less precise and more in keeping with its profound dimensions. In fact, this is the way that the experts present *lectio divina*. Here are a few examples: "'Listen' to Christ who speaks through the Scriptures" (B. Baroffio), or even, "Try to 'taste' God" (P.-J. Emery), or another yet: "An astonishing, contemplative reading in which the Word of God reveals to each one, personally, how his own special vocation fits into the convergence of all, towards the one salvation in Christ" (C. Jean-Nesmy). In these expressions the essence of the first and last "times" or steps in *lectio divina* is included, namely *lectio* as hearing (*auditio*) and contemplation (*contemplatio*) as tasting (*gustus*). Other aspects of the truth of *lectio divina* are expressed with a fair approximation if the noun *lectio* (reading) is accompanied by an adjective similar to those proposed by J. Leclercq: "attentive, meditated, prayerful, animated, interior."

The summary, from this point on, of some specific implications will help us to better delineate the characteristics of *lectio divina*.

## 6.1. *Lectio divina* as a full understanding of Scripture

*Lectio divina* recognizes that its first and truly fundamental job is to scrutinize the text of the Bible. The meaning of the word of God is arrived at through a filtering of our understanding of the books which the biblical writers have transmitted to us. For their part, these holy authors belonged to a certain age and culture and they express themselves in a language which is very different from that of those who practice *lectio divina*. To understand the message which God is addressing to

us through the writings of the Bible it is, therefore, necessary to complete some stages which free
the word from the conditioning which comes
from such diversity. It is to this end that biblical
commentaries can and ought to be used in the
practice of *lectio divina.* To omit them, holding
that it is possible to glean the biblical message
from an understanding of the text as it stands in
its obvious literal sense, would be to manifest a
naivete or perhaps even an ignorance of the com-
plexity of the sacred text. After rather lengthy experience, the Fathers of the early Church realized
that the Scriptures were as bountiful as a "forest,"
as vast as the "sea" (St. Gregory the Great), as
extensive as the "heavens" (Rupert of Deutz).
Whoever would ignore their experience and ven-
ture forth without provisions into the immensity
of the Bible is a reckless individual who exposes
himself to the risk of settling for an approximation of the meaning of the text and of gambling
with fundamentalism, two of the worst misfor-
tunes that can befall us in our attempts to understand the Bible.

But there is also another risk: that, perhaps
unconscious, of attributing to the books which
make up the Bible different values, and as a consequence of this to imagine that the New Testament and in particular the words of Jesus are more

exhaustively *the* "word of God" than those which are found in other books or passages of Scripture. It is not easy to escape this temptation if we are forced to confront texts which dryly recount the census of the Israelites in the desert of Sinai with which the book of Numbers begins, with a Gospel parable, so rich in its theological and spiritual message, as that of Luke's parable of the prodigal son. Even some theologians who — in simply trying to explain some difficulties in the biblical text — deny that some passages of the Bible were divinely inspired (e.g., Tb 11:4 or 2 Tm 4:13) have fallen into this temptation. This temptation leads, even today, to a very grave error: that of imagining that in the Bible there are some texts richer in divine inspiration than others and that, as a consequence, these are, more than the others, the "word of God." It was in reference to this problem that the Second Vatican Council, reiterating the teachings of the Council of Trent and of the First Vatican Council, affirmed: "Holy Mother Church, relying on the faith of the apostolic age, accepts as sacred and canonical the books of the Old and New Testaments, whole and entire, with all their parts, on the grounds that, written under the inspiration of the Holy Spirit, they have God as their author" (*Dei Verbum*, 11).

If, then, God is the "author" of all the Bible

it follows that He is making a single discourse from the beginning to the end of it. Thus *lectio divina*, while concentrating on a fragment of the Bible, listens to the whole discourse which God is making in the Scriptures. And it listens to all of its echoes. From time to time, these present themselves, one with respect to another, as an anticipation or illumination and conclusion, but it is only in their differentiation and complementarity that they constitute the fullness of the word of God. Even the marginal references, present in all the better editions of the Bible and always to be consulted, teach. To this fullness of listening are dedicated those "times" of the *lectio* and *meditatio* in the practice of *lectio divina*. It happens, then, that often a tiny biblical passage reveals something of greater and more profound significance and introduces into a single part of the word another word of God.

St. Gregory the Great has handed down to us his own experience which has entered into the history of the practice of *lectio divina*: "The divine word grows along with those who read it." The early Fathers lived their encounter with the Bible as listeners who enriched themselves from its infinite patterns. Their experience remains paradigmatic and perennially valid.

## 6.2. *Lectio divina* as an understanding of Scripture in an ecclesial context

From the fact that it is indispensable to refer to the explanation of biblicists, it does not follow that these provide all that *lectio divina* can expect from the word of God. *Lectio divina* seeks to listen to the word not only in the globality with which it resonates in the text of Scripture, but also in the fullness with which it has been understood in Christian times, and hence in the tradition of the Church. This is personified in an excellent manner by the Fathers of the Church. In fact "the Christian life — that is, the salvific experience of the mystery of Christ expressed in the living testimony and cultural reflection of Christians — does not cease with the conclusions of New Testament revelation, but has enjoyed a continuation in the ecclesial community" (A. Amato). The Fathers taught the exegetes and Christians of all times to accept the Scriptures in their entirety and to go through them without losing themselves in their obscurity or in their details, always directing themselves to Christ. For the ability to guide to this encounter the Fathers are truly "masters in the interpretation of the Scriptures" (A. Benoit).

Today, more than ever, the assertion of St.

Augustine — who gives credit to the Fathers who had preceded him by not many years — that the Fathers were "masters" of the Church and inspirers of "true wisdom and authentic Christianity" has proved to be true. The scriptural interpretations of the Fathers "retain a permanent value" and the spiritual-theological synthesis put together by them "lies at the center not only of every Christian exegesis, but also of the Christian faith itself" (H. de Lubac). The theological and spiritual dimensions of the interpretative efforts of the Fathers are directed to an encounter with "the Beloved who comes to the garden of his bride" (Sg 5:1; J.-R. Bouchet). It is right, then, to speak of the "grace of the Fathers" (Y.-M. Congar). These considerations were behind the actual rediscovery of the Fathers as masters of the interpretation of Sacred Scripture.

*Lectio divina*, being guided to find in Scripture the nourishment which the divine word is to the faith, brings to fruition the works of the Fathers; hence its practitioners have recourse to the Fathers to be led in their growth in faith. *Lectio divina* also seeks in the writings of the Fathers those paths that lead to love which they have joined together with those of faith, as the medieval saying indicates: "Love is knowledge." In fact there exists a certain reciprocity between faith and love: faith generates love and love invigorates faith. Faith is the path to love. Love is the path to faith. Nothing is more loved than that which is believed. *Lectio divina* looks to the Fathers for enlightenment in order to enter into the profound dimensions of the word of God and for guidance to learn its secrets, following the paths of faith and love which they had taken.

## 6.3. *Lectio divina* as spiritual reading, reading "in the Spirit"

Referring to Scripture and to the commentaries of the Fathers leads us to recall the presence and the activity of the Holy Spirit. The relationship of the Spirit to the Scriptures and to the Fathers lies on two different planes: in the first case, in fact, the Spirit acts in that He has "inspired" the Scriptures; in the other case, the Spirit acts in that He has "enlightened" the Fathers to recognize in the Scriptures that which He has "inspired" in them. Given these distinctions, the action of the Spirit remains a fact.

For this reason *lectio divina* also seeks the "spiritual sense" of Scripture. The "spiritual sense" is not that which is produced by an allegorism uprooted from the biblical text, the fruit of fantasy, or a lucubration lacking all criteria. The "spiritual sense" is the literal sense of the text which, all the same, does not always totally exhaust the meaning of the text. In every case, in order to enter into the fullness of the text, the inspiration of the Spirit on the spirit of the one who practices *lectio divina* is necessary. In fact, the meaning of the Bible comes from a higher dimension than that of the unaided human intelligence — a faculty which can probably arrive on its own to an understanding of the whole thought of a human writer. It can even help in understanding the Scriptures in a superior way to that of simple information and abstract knowledge. But to know the things of God requires the Spirit of God: in fact "no one has ever been able to know the secrets of God except the Spirit of God" (1 Cor 2:11); for it is "the Spirit who scrutinizes everything, even the depths of God" (1 Cor 2:10).

*Lectio divina* requires, then, that the one who practices it be fully open and totally at the disposition of the Spirit. Scripture has in itself the grace of possessing, over and above the obvious sense, a special spiritual resonance which only a mind enlightened by the Spirit is able to recognize and only an ear open to the Spirit is able to perceive. Besides, biblical language possesses the capacity to evoke a response by means of which it is able to say more than what the words in themselves say.

The words of the Bible speak, besides through that which they mean, also through that which they suggest. They are in fact the word of God, which is not exhausted certainly in the writings of a book, even one as unique and holy as the Bible. When *lectio divina* is truly a "reading in the Spirit," that is enlightened and guided by the Holy Spirit, the words of the Bible reveal "something more" than what they signify (J. Leclercq): that which the Word expresses, but also that which lies hidden within the Word.

The lives of the saints convey examples of how *lectio*, if one is open to the enlightenment and suggestions of the Spirit, enriches the message. St. Thérèse of Lisieux has given us a record of how she came to recognize love as her special vocation: from the *lectio* of chapter twelve of the First Letter to the Corinthians, she realized that not to everyone was granted the grace to be "apostles, prophets, doctors, etc.": this discovery did not dampen her "desires." So she persisted in seeking in the Scriptures the answer which she needed. She succeeded in finding it when, "bent over" like Mary Magdalene at the entrance of the tomb of Jesus (cf. Jn 20:11) — that is trying to enter into the biblical text — "she ended, like the Magdalene, in finding that which she sought." She learned from 1 Cor 12:31 that "love is the more excellent way," that "only love causes the members of the Church to act"; that it is love that propelled the apostles to preach the Gospel, the martyrs to shed their blood, and so forth. Thus she obtained the enlightenment that she sought: "Love encompasses all vocations, love is everything, love embraces all times and all places." And she concluded: "Finally I found my vocation: my vocation is love"; "I have found my place in the Church": "In the heart of the Church I will be love."

A simple *lectio* of the Pauline text reveals that the Apostle is really dealing with other themes: the presence, the diversity and the utility of charisms in the Church. Entrusted to the Spirit, in the spirit of St. Thérèse this exegetical *lectio* took on "little by little" a fuller sense, it came to assume a meaning that is in the text but which goes beyond the text. In fact the charism presents itself as gift, the Spirit is revealed as love, the Church is presented as the place of one's own personal vocation, one's personal vocation is defined as one's special place in the Church, love is seen as that which unifies all of them. Said in another way: love is recognized by St. Thérèse as her very personal gift of the Spirit for her place in the Church.

Once again it is true that "the word of God grows along with those who read it," with those who keep up a dialogue of love with it, with the heart that allows itself to be touched by it. Truly "the Spirit touches the spirit of the reader," as St. Gregory the Great so wisely taught.

# The prayer of *"lectio divina"*

A fundamental characteristic of *lectio divina* is the combination of an ancient form with actual prayer. This aspect can be seen both in the meaning and in the practice of *lectio divina*.

## 1. The demands of prayer

Today we find a strong demand for prayer and for prayer which is authentic. The *oratio* of *lectio divina* offers a response to this demand.

### 1.1. The presence of prayer

A basic element in the encounter of the believer with God, prayer figures into the religious writings of Buddhists and Muslims and invests all their specific expressions. In the books of the Old Testament prayer is presented in two forms: personal, of which the Psalms are a splendid manifestation, and communitarian which the Jews celebrated in the courtyard of the Temple in Jerusalem and in the synagogues of their cities. Even in the New Testament and in early Christianity these two fundamental forms are represented. Personal prayer: "Pray at all times in the Spirit with every manner of prayer and supplication. To this end stay alert and persevere in supplication on behalf of all the saints" (Eph 6:18). "Therefore my desire is that at every place the men should lift holy hands in prayer without anger or arguing. Likewise, the women" (1 Tm 2:8-9).

Already in the New Testament and with total clarity in the earliest Christian writings prayer in a communitarian form is presented. The very ancient writing (1st century) entitled the *Didaché: The Teaching of the Twelve Apostles* prescribes (cc. 8-10) that Christians not only recite the "Our Father" and intercede for the Church, but it refers also to the very ancient text of a eucharistic celebration, woven throughout with biblical references. Clement of Alexandria (+ 210) urges those who want to be Christians to take part in those meetings where hymns and psalms are prayed and to participate in the "conversations on the Scriptures." This is certainly an interesting piece of data for *lectio divina*, as is his recommendation for the chronological ordering of events: "before dinner" or "before going to bed at night." Although generic, these reminders show us a very ancient form of *lectio divina* in which the *lectio* is linked to the *oratio*.

## 1.2. Some lights on prayer

Undoubtedly the practice of prayer has never declined among Christians, nor could it: it, in fact, constitutes the very nearly only way which permits a religious person to realize his or her undeniable and never fully satisfied desire to enter into contact with God. Notwithstanding this, or perhaps precisely because of this, prayer has its own history. This accounts for the inexhaustible research of ever new ways to live prayer be it in a communitarian form — that of the public and liturgical prayer of the Church which as far back as the 2nd century St. Justin defined as "a house of prayer and adoration" — or in a personal form, which Origen early understood as a "listening" to God and making room for the Holy Spirit "who intercedes unceasingly for us with unutterable sighs." These forms of prayer have followed, down the centuries, their own paths which cannot all be recalled here, but which have had articulations which coincide with the historical-cultural movements of the monastic Middle Ages, the Renaissance, the Enlightenment and obviously, those of modern times.

The definitions of prayer are as many as are the instructors who have taught it. All the same the paths identified and followed converge on certain essential facts and sources of prayers. Cassian (4th century) expressed this, saying that there is prayer when "every love, every desire, every undertaking, every effort, every thought, the whole of our life and our picture of future bliss is God"; we pray when we are "united to God by a perpetual and indivisible love, when we are united to him to the point where all that we feel, think and say are God alone."

Some centuries later, St. Francis de Sales (in 1616) wrote this of prayer which above all reflects the teaching of St. Gregory of Nyssa: "Prayer is a colloquy and a conversation of the soul with God." Then, explaining that aspect of prayer which is not only dialogical but also inspirational, he went on to say: "If prayer is a colloquy, a dialogue, a conversation, then through it we speak to God and God in turn speaks to us; we aspire (*aspirare*) to be with Him and breathe (*respirare*) in Him and reciprocally He inspires (*inspirare*) us and breathes (*respirare*) on us." St. Francis de Sales goes farther and sets forth the fundamental components of prayer: "Of what do we speak in prayer? What is the subject of our colloquy? Optimally, we speak only of God. In fact of whom could love speak or carry on a conversation if not with the Beloved?" Comparing speculative and mystical theology he deduced another aspect regarding prayer calling it a "conversation" with God: "It is absolutely secret and in it nothing is said between God and the soul if not heart-to-heart, with a communication that cannot be shared by anyone else outside of those who initiate it. The language of lovers is so special that no one can comprehend it except them. Where love reigns, there is no need of spoken words or of the use of the senses to converse and listen one to the other" (*Treatise on the Love of God*, VI, 1).

## 1.3. Some of prayer's shadows

The texts which we have just recalled are full of a heavy cargo of spirituality. It would not surprise us to find this present in the words of Cassian: he, in fact, addressed his teaching to monks. What does surprise us though is that the same robust spirituality is present also in the teachings of St. Francis de Sales who wrote to "every devout soul who wants to make progress." And still this was the way in which Christians of those times were guided on the way of prayer. And so it continued to be for centuries in that the influence of St. Francis de Sales on methods of prayer "lasted significantly up to our own day" (J.A. Jungmann). In Christian times both prayer and the *oratio* of *lectio divina* were set forth and, credibly, also lived in their details. Has this ceased to be? And if so, when and why did this happen?

A profound and also critical rethinking of the subject of prayer took place when those known as "masters of doubt" appeared on the scene. In truth their thought had nothing to do either with the field of theology nor with that which is specifically ascetical and still they came to influence both theology and asceticism through the conduit of modern culture with which Christians cannot be and indeed are not strangers. It will be useful to revisit some of these "doubters" who have contributed to situating prayer in a dimension which is strictly anthropological. Such "doubters" can be lumped together as having three distinct tendencies. The first tendency is of a philosophical character and defines prayer as "superstition," which imagines that prayer has the power to change the course of events; the second is of a psychological nature and criticizes prayer as an "illusion," in which one presumes that God is disposed to make His actions depend on the desires of the one who prays; the third is known as ethical-social in nature and incriminates prayer because it would make those who pray forget their responsibilities in confrontation with the social context. Some references will serve to better detail what we are talking about.

According to I. Kant (1724-1804), since prayer is "a desire manifested to a Being which has no need of any explanation of the inner intentions of the desiring subject," it becomes simply "an interior conversation with oneself, who supposes himself to be conversing very intelligently with God." Hence "prayer, conceived as an interior cult to God and thus as a means of grace, is a superstitious error." Such an anthropological reduction of prayer is represented also in the idealistic philosophy of L. Feuerbach (1804-1872): "Prayer is the unconditional faith of the human heart in the absolute identity of that which is subjective with that which is objective." It follows that "in prayer man adores his own heart, contemplates his own sentiments as a divine being" and hence prayer "duplicates the self in a dialogue with the self, with one's own heart."

Religion understood as a conglomerate of superstitions was transformed by S. Freud (1856-1939) into an "illusion." Considered in their "psychic genesis," "religious representations present themselves as dogmas, but they are illusions, filled with the oldest, strongest, most pressing desires of humanity. The infant's terrible sensation of impotence has caused the need for protection to be born in him — protection through love — which parents provide. The recognition that such impotence lasts throughout the entire course of life has caused the keeping in existence of a father, this time, however, a more powerful Father, namely God the Father. Through the benign governance of divine Providence, the anxieties before the dangers of life are calmed, and the prolongation of terrestrial existence by means of a future life institutes the spatial and temporal structure in which the fulfillment of the desire can take place. It would be truly beautiful if there were a God — Creator of the universe and benevolent Providence — a universal moral order and otherworldly life." These negative considerations about religion inevitably bring with them repercussions on prayer: as in the case of religion, so also prayer is an "illusion," generated by the irrepressible desire of man that reality be as he wants it to be.

The third line of tendencies are described as ethical-social and blame prayer because it would cause those who pray to forget their responsibilities vis-a-vis the social situation. The Anglican Bishop of Woolwich, J.A.T. Robinson, proposed this "non-religious" interpretation of prayer, which would consist not in a search for communion with God, but in dedication to man. He wrote: "The fulcrum of prayer consists in opening oneself unconditionally, in love, to others… in being united to others in the presence of God." In this viewpoint, prayer comes to consist in practical undertakings in favor of others. Following in this direction one comes (along with J.B. Metz, E. Bloch, R.A. Alves and others) to a "political interpretation of the Gospel."

## 1.4. A search for other kinds of prayer

These examples are emblematic of the situation and of the difficulties and tensions in which prayer is debated today. The above mentioned attempts at a solution are debatable and even unacceptable under a Christian profile; in any case they constitute the actual context of the reflections and questions of believers and theologians regarding prayer. But these do not make up the entire scope of the actual problem concerning prayer. There are in fact tendencies of another kind, such as the search for prayer characterized by emotive spontaneity or by esoteric forms of meditation and contemplation.

The dating of contemporary examples can be grouped in two cycles. In the '60's there took place an important critical moment for prayer: under the impulse of critics, these "masters of doubt," cases promoting the purification of prayer — in which prayer was not seen as an ingenuous illusion or a protective psychological duplicity on the part of those who pray or as the projection of a stop-gap God — could be affirmed. In this climate "secular" formulations of prayer came into being. These combined novelty and ambiguity and were disseminated in the form of slogans such as the following: "To pray is to open oneself to others," "My work is my prayer," "All life is a prayer." In the '70's — and this following the Second Vatican Council — there took place a religious revival: a taste for the spontaneity, the ritual and symbolic dimensions of prayer, a hunger for spiritual and religious experience, an interest in the techniques of meditation and prayer coming from the Orient, the charismatic renewal as well as a certain kind of return to intimate mysticism. In response to this complex of examples and aspirations there arose various "schools of prayer." Recalling some facts about them will render more or less apparent the actual course of prayer in these times.

In contrast to the preponderantly rationalistic approach of the West, the form of prayer from the world of the Christian East which went under the name of "the prayer of Jesus" or "the prayer of the heart" belonging to the ascetic and mystical form of hesychasm, which means "re-pose" or "quiet," was reevaluated. This kind of prayer consists in the synchronization of the physical rhythm of one's breathing between the repetitions of a formula such as the traditional, "Lord Jesus, have mercy on me a sinner" or others like it in order to fix one's attention on the presence of Jesus. The quiet repetition by the lips of this sort of "mantra" (characteristic of Buddhism) obtains the shifting of one's prayer from the mind to the heart and leads, thus, to a profound knowledge of the inhabiting presence of Christ with the Father and the Spirit. This technique can help both to enter into prayer and to remain in contemplation.

A similar direction was sought in the discipline of prayer coming from the East and in particular from Hinduism and Buddhism with the goal of creating a sort of Christian yoga. In it certain bodily positions and respiratory techniques are proposed as an aid for disposing oneself to a more profound prayer, withdrawing one from the chaotic world of multiplicity to "recollect" oneself and enter into one's own center, and here in humble adoration to surrender oneself to the divine Word.

Another direction of prayer is represented by the "charismatic movement," present as much in

the Catholic Church now as it is in Protestant-
ism. Its characteristic is to get several people together to praise God, draw instruction from Scripture and the doctrine of the Church, and in general to experience the presence of the Holy Spirit,
as little by little those present make themselves
available in sincerity to allow the charisms of the
Spirit to emerge and to edify the body of Christ.
The choral singing which sets off the times of
prayer, reflects the biblical theme which acts as a
support to the prayer itself.

Following Vatican II other forms of
communitarian prayer, liturgical and non-liturgi-
cal, have also developed with particular attention
to the celebration, even as a family, of Lauds and
Vespers and the "Prayer of the Faithful."

In their desire for prayer contemporary
Christians have, then, rediscovered some techniques proper to the spirituality of the East be it
Christian or non-Christian and have identified
once again, as suggested by the development of
the psychological sciences and characterized by a
reevaluation of communitarian sharing, what offers the best possibilities for expressing the unity
of the persons who are praying. Such methods are
still waiting to be verified as far as the possibility
of leading to a more profound prayer, greater
availability to God and greater charity towards

God and neighbor are concerned. They do, however, run parallel to the *oratio* and the *meditatio* of the *lectio divina*, which, in many ways, preceded them.

## 2. "*Lectio divina*" and prayer

It is impossible to discern the work of illumination, purification and transformation which the word of God and the grace of the Spirit accomplish in the heart and soul of those who dedicate themselves to *lectio divina*. It is instead possible to recognize how in it the *oratio*, assuming in itself many of the characteristics of prayer, proves itself to be rich in authenticity and even responsive to the problems which modernity poses to Christian prayer.

### 2.1. The "*lectio*" for prayer

For reasons of didactic exposition and as well also of practical necessity, it is customary to divide the development of the *lectio divina* into "times," called *lectio, meditatio, oratio* and *contemplatio*. In reality there is only *oratio* since this constitutes the thread that unifies them, the element that is common to them all while respecting the identity of each one. The faith conviction that in the Bible there is a presence of the word of God arouses the disposition to listen to it and infuses the desire to want to be nurtured by it according to the assertion: "Man lives by every word that comes forth from the mouth of God" (Mt 4:4; Dt 8:3). An indispensable condition for keeping such a desire while practicing *lectio divina* is to have an infinite love for the Bible. Faith and love are indispensable conditions for entering into a dialogue with God by means of the word of God. To live *lectio divina* in this way is already prayer.

The *lectio* ends above all in an opening into that dialogue which is *oratio*. Whoever practices *lectio divina* prays during the "time" of the *lectio* through a tranquil, prolonged and peaceful listening to God in His word. The first attitude required by this form of *oratio* consists in presenting oneself to God in unarmed poverty. Those who practice *lectio divina* have nothing to say to God, not even something to ask of Him, even if they expect much from Him. He will ask of God what he will hear from God; if he asks something of Him, it will be that which the word of God will have made known to him as something necessary or useful. In the meantime he will dedicate himself to listening and to making himself available to be taught, enriched, enlightened and inspired.

The *lectio* is *oratio* even in the apprehension of the word of God which takes place through the patient and prolonged repetition of it. Such repetition gives rise to a possession of those biblical passages learned "by heart" which lead to a possession of a great familiarity with the word of God and contributes to the formation of a biblical mentality, but also, and above all, in appropriating the "*memoria Dei*," an uninterrupted recollection of God and of the sweet sense of His presence. A splendid icon of this way of praying is the Mother of the Lord, who "kept all these things (the events and words of the birth of Christ), meditating on them in her heart" (Lk 2:19). In such a way the "time" of the *lectio* becomes a memorial prayer, or more, an encounter with the Father by means of the Word, who continually reminds us of Him.

## 2.2. The "*meditatio*" as prayer

The prayer dimension is very strong in the "time" of the *meditatio*. It is here that the word listened to becomes "ruminated on" not only with the idea of learning something more, but above all in order to get to the bottom of it, listening to its echoes which are stirred up thanks to the light and the grace of the Spirit, and to assimilate it so that it becomes nourishment of the spirit of the one who practices *lectio divina* and the word of his or her own prayer.

The *meditatio* is the time to rest in the word, to inhabit it as one's own homeland, to put down one's tent in it. It is the time to live it with one's mind and heart, allowing it to descend from the mind which knows it to the heart which welcomes it. This is possible in *meditatio* because it has to do with a word which is not the verbal dictation of a revelation made to a single person as happened in the Koran, nor is it the fruit of speculation on the tradition of ancient sages as took place in the books of the Vedas. The Bible, in fact, narrates the involvement of God in a history which reaches its apex in the Incarnation of the Word, and its traces, written in the Bible and animated by the Spirit, can be retraced by everyone. Whoever, in faith, surrenders to the mystery of the word of God will see that He continues to speak; whoever places himself in an attitude of listening, will hear His voice even if it has no sound.

Where water flows forth there is a spring; where a voice is heard, there is a presence (A.-M. Bernard). If one speaks to me, he is present and his voice, for the fact of its reaching me, draws me to him. A similar thing happens with the word of

God, and the *meditatio* is the effort put forth to establish contact, or at least to render it possible in a less confused manner. *Meditatio* is the attempt to render oneself firmly attentive to the word. So it is necessary to remain "in the fields of the Scriptures," to dedicate oneself to discerning in them the words of Him who "has no form" and yet has a "voice" (cf. Dt 4:12), to examine the echoes of that Voice and to make an effort to recognize in the words Him who pronounces them, thus making the identification: word-voice-Word.

Such was the spiritual path taken by the Israelites of old, when they recognized Yahweh in the voice which on Sinai presented itself only in the sound of thunder (Ex 19:16-19), and from the woman of Magdala when, on Easter morning, she recognized the Risen One in the voice of the gardener who said to her, "Mary" (cf. Jn 20:14-16). The heart made sensitive by the Word and by the Spirit becomes capable of knowing Him who speaks. And also to encounter Him; an encounter, shadowy perhaps, but all the same true. This is already prayer, and authentic prayer: a dialogue entered into with the Voice without a voice, and yet the voice of a presence.

A voice is perceptible because it is made up of vibrations which the ear can pick up as sound when it manages to tune in to its wavelength; in fact, we do not hear ultrasound precisely because we lack the capacity to tune in to its wavelength. Something similar happens even with the word of God: it reaches us, but in order for it to be heard we must be attuned to its wavelength. The capacity or incapacity of tuning in explains how words, subversive of values so admired and sought by the generality of persons, such as the evangelical beatitudes, could have found, down the centuries, so many listeners and followers and equally as many thoughtless individuals and even adversaries. To explain this it is not enough to recognize the sublimity of the message that they proclaim. The fact is that the beatitudes reveal Him who, before pronouncing them, personified them in Himself. He caused them to be heard by the vibrations which came forth from Himself who is at the same time the One who announced the Kingdom, the Messiah, the Word and the Son of God. Listening to the Word of God is possible when one is able to tune into the wavelength not only of the words in themselves but of Him who pronounces them. Offering room to this possibility, *meditatio* becomes *oratio*: a time of tuning in, a time of listening, a time of welcoming Him who is the Voice without sound.

Tuning in to the divine word arouses in the believer the desire to echo the voice which has reached him and to respond to the voice which has touched him. *Meditatio* is transformed, in this way and very naturally, into *oratio*, into prayer which is voice responding to Voice, voice which turns to God guided by the truth which has enlightened it in order to express that it does not find better words than those which it has heard from God. Thus it happens that *oratio* expresses what is heard in the *meditatio* and the best words for expressing it are the same words which were heard; that is, you should pray making your own the words of God: pray to God with the word of God.

That which the early Fathers taught will happen: *meditatio* consists in taking oneself to the "well of Jacob to draw water, which then will well up in *oratio*" (Anonymous, 13th century). This is a characteristic which defines the *oratio* of *lectio divina* and distinguishes it from the usual types of prayer and ennobles the prayer itself.

Guigo II, the Carthusian (12th century) taught in his celebrated booklet, *Jacob's Ladder*, the order of the "times" of *lectio divina*: on the first rung, and hence at the bottom, there is the *lectio*, that is the reading of the biblical text, the discovery of its message, the listening to the "voice" which is expressed by the writing; at the summit stands the *oratio* and the *contemplatio*, the encounter and communion with God. The *meditatio* is found on the intermediate rungs, that is, it is placed as an element which introduces one into the *oratio* and gives rise to *contemplatio*, joining the *lectio* with the *oratio*. In the *meditatio* the fruit which is expressed as a dialogue with God in the *oratio* and as an encounter with him in the *contemplatio* matures.

## 2.3. Prayer as dialogue

Though we are used to personal prayer as a monologue — that is, one in which we alone speak — it is characteristic of Christian prayer that it be a dialogue. All the same this dialogical character must not be mythologized: if in fact the one who prays many times uses words which have a sound, the words which God speaks never have a sound. In fact they are not "words" but "*the* Word," precisely because the Word of God addresses them to us through the Holy Scriptures. Thus, by means of the word, a dialogue is established, which unites the two parts of prayer: the *lectio* is our listening to God in His word, the *oratio* is our response to what God is saying.

A universal implication of *lectio divina* is that it is a dialogue: "A reading done by two" (P. Dumortier) in a "dialogue" in which the communication takes place through that realism of words which are "signs" of love. In such a dialogue the first to speak is God, who — in the *lectio* — speaks to us word-signs of love which He addresses to us through the Word in Sacred Scripture. And the first to listen to such word-signs of love is the one who gives ear to them in the *meditatio*. When this takes place, *lectio divina* approaches its truest *raison d'être*, becoming that kind of colloquy which is prayer: in fact "in the *lectio* God speaks to us, in the *oratio* we speak to God" (Adalgar, 10th century). And as our *oratio* causes the *lectio divina* to approach its *raison d'être*, those who practice it also grow in their own spiritual identity: "*Lectio* and *oratio*, in their alternation render the soul pure and strong, spurred on, as it were, by desire for God" (St. Basil).

Such is the experience of whoever, in ancient times no less than in those more recent, has practiced *lectio divina* in it most authentic way: "Intimate colloquy" and a search "in the bottom of the heart, in the most perfect silence, for the face of the Beloved" (Jerome), in a never interrupted "dialogue of the Spouse with the spouse who seek each other, call out to each other, approach each other" (J. Leclercq). In some privileged cases these even reach that mystical encounter which Origen describes symbolically and poetically in this way: "The soul enters into the mysteries of the wisdom and the knowledge of the Word, as into the nuptial bed of its celestial Spouse," and it "receives the kiss of its Spouse, that is of the Word of God," and it is the "truest, most intimate, most holy [kiss] that the Word gives to His Beloved, to the pure and perfect soul."

It is in the context of these aspirations and expectations that the *oratio* of *lectio divina* has been lived from most ancient times. St. Ambrose recalls the dialogical dimension: "We speak with Christ when we pray; we listen to Him when we read the writings inspired by God." St. Jerome recalls the dialogical and at the same time prayerful dimension of *lectio divina*: "In the *lectio* it is the Spouse who speaks to the soul; in the *oratio* it is the soul that speaks to its Spouse"; "Do you pray? You are speaking to your Spouse. Do you read? It is He who speaks to you." "Whoever wants to remain always with God must dedicate himself frequently to the *oratio* and to the *lectio*." "The *lectio* teaches what to ask for in the *oratio*; after the *oratio* it is necessary to seek in the *lectio* what else to ask for in the *oratio*" (Leander, 6th century). "The *lectio* must serve the *oratio*, to prepare for love. In the *lectio* one learns about Christ; in the *oratio* one enters into a familiar conversation with Him" (Gilbert of Holland, 12th century).

From St. Jerome's viewpoint the *lectio* and the *oratio* constitute the two fundamental aspects of the dialogue of prayer, of the conversation with the Spouse; and he had a strong predilection for it (D. Gorce). He wrote enthusiastically to Eustochium, the first young Roman noblewoman to have chosen consecrated virginity: "The spouse of Christ is like the bow in the rainbow, clothed in gold inside and out (cf. Ex 25:10), guardian of the law of God. Read the Gospel (cf. Lk 10:38-42). Mary, who sat at the feet of Jesus, is preferred to Martha, who was busy about many things. Be like Mary: sit at the feet of Jesus and say: 'I have found Him whom my soul was seeking; I will never leave Him again.' And may He respond to you: 'One alone is my dove' (cf. Sg 3:4; 6:9)."

## 2.4. The word of God and the prayer of man

We are used to formulating prayers with the use of words; they are either pronounced aloud or at least expressed in the mind. Still they are always words which reflect our thoughts, desires which mirror our feelings. *Lectio divina* not only leads to the prayer of dialogue, but it also furnishes the *oratio* with words "that allow the soul to open itself to the Spouse, to manifest to Him the ardor of its love for Him." The soul "finds in the Scriptures the language on which to model the words to manifest to the Spouse the various movements of its heart. At times it expresses the desire to adhere more intimately to Him and the joy which it has in following Him; at times it manifests its fears in the time of temptation. Deriving, therefore, from the *meditatio* on the Scriptures there is first of all the initiation of an easy-going colloquy and then the possibility of maintaining it" (D. Gorce).

The much-used medieval Latin works, the *Florilegia*, bear witness to the conviction that the Scriptures can offer words to our prayer. These books are collections in which the monks recopied the biblical texts which they had enjoyed during *lectio divina* so that they could return to them again to relish and make them the object of new meditations and other prayers: "Like the bees, the monks brought together in such books the nectar and pollen [of their *lectio divina*] in order to fashion a unique comb of honey" (J. Leclercq), that of their *oratio*.

The teachings which come from Christian and monastic antiquity about the utility of the Word of God to formulate our *oratio* have been set forth again in didactic and up-to-date language by M. Magrassi:

To express ourselves to God there is no more facile and secure a way than to read, listen, ruminate on the word, and then to repeat back to God that which He has said to us, transfusing into those words all of one's thought, all of one's love and all of one's life.

To pray, it is not necessary to rack the brain to artificially provoke interior acts, thoughts, and super-fine affections, but rather to respond when faced by the biblical text with a free and spontaneous prayer. And when this spontaneous effusion ceases, to return to the text to be replenished anew with nourishment.

Too often prayer dies on one's lips or takes refuge in formulae mechanically repeated. Or, if one insists in pressuring the interior faculties, it fluctuates between arid reasoning and sentimental dreaming. Lacking nourishment, it functions on empty. For this there is but one remedy: nourish your prayer with all that rich deposit which the word, read in silence, has left in us. There we find irresistible words, which go directly to the heart of God; from there we are able to change the accents to express to God the various movements of our heart. And when the aridity of our heart does not let us do otherwise, it will be enough to repeat to God, in vocal form, that which He Himself has said to us, after having brought mind and heart into harmony.

St. Augustine already presented us with a teaching similar to that of Magrassi when he exhorted us in an extremely concise way to "say nothing to God apart from Him."

## 2.5. Prayer: being with God

With the goal of stirring up the fervor of the Carthusians of Mont-Dieu (in the Ardenne mountains of France) the mystical theologian William of Saint-Thierry (12th century) wrote them his *Golden Letter*, in which he expresses a fundamental element of prayer: "To pray is to remain tranquil in spirit in order to enjoy God for as long a time as possible."

From the *lectio* of the Bible the *oratio* learns to "remain" with God. The prolongation of this "remaining" leads to a communion which is true prayer. When this happens, the one who prays enters into a peaceful state in which he can "enjoy God." In such a way the *oratio*, starting with the word of God, articulates itself in a dialogue and develops as a "remaining with God" in a sign of love, arriving at its apex which takes place surely in *contemplatio*, but which has its beginning during the time of *meditatio* and unfolds in that intimate conversation which is the *oratio* itself.

Placing the one who prays in continual contact with the word of God, *lectio divina* constitutes a splendid school not only of *oratio*, but also, more generally, in the itinerary of the soul to God. In the highly celebrated letter to Eustochium, his "daughter, disciple and sister," St. Jerome describes, in a dramatic and at the same time lyrical form, the journey in which, moving from *lectio divina*, he was leading the young virgin first to recognize the voice of the Spouse and then to encounter Him:

> In the *oratio* you speak to the Spouse; in the *lectio* the Spouse speaks to you. When, according to the command of the Lord (Mt 6:6), you have prayed to your Father in secret, the Spouse will come and knock at the door and say: "Behold, I stand at the door and knock; if anyone hears my voice and opens the door, I will enter and dine with him and he with me" (Rv 3:20). You, with great eagerness, will say: "It is the voice of my Beloved," and immediately you will get

up and let Him in. He will enter and sup with you and you with Him. And when sleep overtakes you, the Spouse will come to the walls of your room: then you will arise, all trembling, and say: "I am faint with love" (Sg 5:8).

## 2.6. Prayer for "*contemplatio*"

Explaining a very difficult text from the Prophet Ezekiel (1:19) relative to the vision of the "chariot of the Lord" and in particular to the movement of its "wheels" and to the presence of "living beings," St. Gregory the Great — identifying the "wheels" with the words of the Bible and the "living beings" with the readers thereof — finds a way to teach in some way how the words of Scripture lead to *contemplatio*:

> The "living beings" arise from the earth when they hang suspended in *contemplatio*. To the measure in which each one progresses personally even Sacred Scripture makes progress in him because the divine word grows along with the one who reads it; in fact one understands that much more profoundly the more profoundly he pays attention to the word addressed to him.

For this reason if the living beings do not rise from earth, neither do the "wheels" arise, because if the soul of the reader does not tend on high, the divine words, not understood, remain earthbound. When the sense of the word of God seems to leave the one who reads it tepid, when the language of Scripture does not inflame his soul and does not cause some resplendent meaning to dance in his soul, even the "wheels" remain inert on earth, because the living being does not rise from earth.

If instead the "living being" moves, that is if it seeks ways of living well, then at the same time the "wheels" also move because from the divine word you will draw that much greater profit the more the progress you have realized in confronting the word. If, then, the "living being," taking wing, strains toward contemplation, the "wheels" immediately lift off from the earth, because you understand that those things are not earthbound which previously in the word of God were held to be spoken in an earthly way. You feel that the words of Sacred Scripture are heavenly if, having received the grace of *contemplatio*, you rush towards celestial realities. And when the soul of the reader is penetrated with love for things supernal, then it feels the wonderful and ineffable power of the word of God.

Thus it happens that the knowledge of the Scriptures and *contemplatio* influence one another: the Scriptures understood in the Spirit lead to *contemplatio*; the light of *contemplatio* leads to a more informed understanding of the Scriptures.

## 2.7. Prayer for action ("*operatio*")

One can easily agree that the word of God leads to *contemplatio*, but it may seem that in *lectio divina* parts of contemporary prayer which are very strongly felt are absent, namely for example, *oratio* and above all *contemplatio* combined with concrete Christian commitment. St. Bonaventure would respond (in his *Legenda maior*) to this problem by recalling St. Francis. While considering himself a "fool," that is, as one deprived of a "competence in Sacred Scripture," nonetheless Francis was able "to penetrate the maze of its mysteries" because "he read the holy books and once he had entered into their mentality, he tenaciously inscribed them in his memory, so that that which he had not in vain collected with his attentive mind he pondered continuously with loving devotion." Thus it happened that "love allowed him to enter where the science of the masters stopped." From *lectio divina* Francis learned that, according to the Gospel, Jesus "prayed more than He read." For this reason he saw to it that his friars "did not neglect to apply themselves to prayer and that they studied not so much to know how to speak, but to put into practice what they had learned and, after having practiced it, to propose it also to the action of others."

In the homily mentioned earlier Gregory the Great found a way of teaching the relationship between *lectio divina* and the duties of the Christian life with a series of variations on the text which says: "The spirit of life was in the wheels" (Ezk 1:20), by showing how the first operative fruit of the word of God was the interior transformation of its reader: "The spirit of life is in the 'wheels' because with the gift of the Spirit by means of the word of God, we receive life." "One can understands that the spirit moves, when in various ways and degrees God touches the soul of the reader." "The Spirit touches the soul of the reader so that it might become capable of compunction, patience, and be dedicated to preaching."

The concern of the contemporaneous "moving" and "halting" of the "living beings" and of the "wheels" (Ezk 1:21), offers a way for the pope, monk and biblical scholar to expound also on the multiform Christian duties required by the word of God:

> Some go forward in that they know how to administer well the goods they have received, taking care of the works of mercy, bringing aid to the oppressed. These "move" in the sense that they tend toward the service of their neighbor. The "wheels," then, move with them, because the divine word guides their steps on the road to their neighbor. Others are so strong in keeping the faith they have received that they confront all adversity, and not only do they not allow themselves to be overcome by the perversity of incredulity, but they combat those who sustain errors and bring them back to the right way: with these the "wheels" are also immovable and the words of Sacred Scripture confirm their constancy. Others, in the end, turn their back on the things of earth and ignoring all that happens fix themselves on the *contemplatio* of God. With these who are lifted on high, the "wheels" also arise, because in the measure in which one progresses on high the divine words also speak to him of more elevated things.

Gregory concludes: "The 'living beings,' then, go forward in the service of the neighbor, they stop in guarding personal steadfastness, they arise toward the contemplation of God. But even the 'wheels' go forward, stop, and arise: in fact in Sacred Scripture we find what we become. Have you moved toward an active live? Sacred Scripture moves along with you. Have you reached a certain consistency and stability of spirit? The Scriptures halt with you. Have you arrived, by the grace of God, at a life of contemplation? The Scriptures take wing with you. [...] In this way the Scriptures become for us in the darkness of the present life, the light to our path."

## 2.8. The *"oratio"* as total prayer

The contemporary examples of new ways of prayer are characterized as dialogue, prayer of the heart, meditative prayer, prayer in the Spirit in order to encounter God in love, commitment to the service of one's neighbor in love. All of these examples are implicit in the various "times" of *lectio divina*: they trace an itinerary which begins with a *lectio* of the Scriptures and, moving upward step by step, lead toward an encounter with God.

Recalling the "times" of *lectio divina*, the spontaneous flow of one into the other lies behind the sign of their oneness: what precedes would be lost without that which follows, and that which follows would be inconsistent without that which precedes. One understands, then, how *lectio divina* is prayer in its overall development. Each of its "times" is such in a specific way — listening to God through His word, welcoming it, dialoguing, encountering, witnessing — and the sum of its "times" results in the fact that *lectio divina* is in its entirety *oratio*. Prayer, in fact, is listening, welcoming, dialoguing, encountering God and commitment to the things of God. *Lectio divina* incorporates the best components of prayer. *Lectio divina* is authentic prayer, prayer which combines in itself all the components of prayer.

Many are the questions that are asked of Christian prayer and many are the ways of responding which are sought today. But many also are the responses offered by *lectio divina*, if lived in the multiple possibilities which it allows, such as *oratio*. Turning our attention to the prospects opened up by *lectio divina* the medieval monk, Gottfried of Admont, wrote: "If we love to drink the wine of Sacred Scripture with our spiritual intelligence, we will know how to make of it our food through the understanding of our hearts, and will see arise over us the radiant morning of God."

# The practice of *"lectio divina"*

The considerations covered up to here are meant to be a preface to an outline of some convictions with regard to the word of God and to give some introduction to the practice of *lectio divina*. Everything we do is, in fact, the consequence of that which we believe.

From this point on some very concrete suggestions regarding the practice of *lectio divina* will be proposed. They are culled from ancient monastic traditions, but they also dip, in part, into my long acquaintanceship with the Scriptures and from the many and varied experiences I have had with *lectio divina*. The suggestions which follow are directed above all to those who practice *lectio divina* in common, but they will be found useful, substantially, with a few minor variations, even by those who practice them in a personal way. In both cases there is place for the imagination, the creativity and the good taste of each one.

## 1. The place

*Lectio divina* is an eminently meditative and prayerful practice: hence it should be practiced in a place which permits silence and favors recollection, reflection and prayer.

For the place, an ordinary room suitable for cultural or spiritual use could be chosen. This might be outfitted with appropriate furniture: the book of the word of God (the Bible or liturgical Lectionary) prominently displayed (e.g., on a stand or table); a lighted candle, symbol and reminder of the risen Christ who makes Himself present anew in His word and a sign of our faith in Him and in it; an icon, preferably Christological; sufficient lighting for reading and at the same time not so bright that it becomes distracting. Some means for providing background music might be helpful, if it can be introduced without too much trouble.

## 2. The time

The time to practice *lectio divina* should be chosen so as not to pressure the participants with a sense of urgency; the quiet required to live the various "times" of *lectio divina* comes from a freedom from restrictions imposed by personal or community commitments. For this reason, but also for the fact of being occupied, from the rising of the sun to its setting, with mundane affairs, and for the need to take into consideration those psychological dispositions which favor concentration on the essentials and on being disposed to communicate with God, the hours between dusk and nightfall seem from experience to be the most suitable for the practice of *lectio divina*.

### 3. The duration

The duration of *lectio divina* must respond to two needs: it must allow for the tranquil development of all its "times" and safeguard the participants from effort and fatigue. To go beyond these limits would be to cause damage to the efficacy of *lectio divina*. The duration must, therefore, take into consideration the capacities and the possibilities of the participants and the requirements of *lectio divina*.

Experience teaches that a communal *lectio divina* can not be undertaken tranquilly in less than an hour, and that it becomes fatiguing if it goes on longer than two hours. If possible, it would be good to organize it in such a way that not all the time has to be spent in the same place and in the same position: if there is an appropriate space nearby (a cloister, park, garden, church or something similar), the assembly could break up temporarily and the participants be given freedom to move to those areas for the "times" of *contemplatio* and even that of personal *oratio*.

## 4. The participants

Participants don't have to have any special cultural level: the word of God and the *lectio divina* are, in fact, for all. All the same, it is very helpful if the *lectio* and the *meditatio* are initiated by a person who has been adequately prepared. All the participants in *lectio divina* will derive more benefit if the interpretation of Scripture is well presented and if they get off to a good start in deepening their theological-spiritual understanding of it.

As for the participants in communitarian *lectio divina*, experience teaches that the optimal number revolves around fifteen: such a number is sufficient to constitute a real community but it also avoids the problem of having some feel lost or anonymous in the group; such a number also allows the participation of several voices in the *collatio*. It is also helpful if the communitarian

*lectio divina* is presided over by one of the participants who, however, limits himself or herself to
coordinating the flow of the various "times."

## 5. Preparation

The composition of an atmosphere fit for
the development of *lectio divina* is important, but
of fundamental importance is the disposition
which each one brings to its participation. From
the current teachings of Christian tradition regarding the *lectio* of Scripture, we recall but a few.

First of all, "purity of heart" understood as
freedom from preconceptions of the word of God.
Whoever, in fact, would prepare to participate in
*lectio divina* under the influence of preconceptions
would find himself hindered in offering a free, dis-
armed listening to what God, by means of His
word, wants to communicate. He would be in-
duced to find in the word that which,
preconceptually, he thought he would find there.
And he would fall into the mistake of substitut-
ing his own "word" for the word of God, while
wanting to listen to God and not to himself. According to St. Bernard, only to a heart thus puri-
fied from such preconceptions does "Wisdom give
itself."

And it is likewise necessary to perform on

oneself a work of "decantation." We are used to a whirlwind of diverse thoughts and sentiments: we have, then, to lay down the dredges of our heart on the bank of our lives and replace them with waters which are less agitated. But it is also necessary to liberate ourselves from the impression of being too much at home, of taking it easy, because in this way the will gets soft.

It is also essential to place oneself in rapport with the sacred text in an attitude "of love" (C. Péguy), in the knowledge that "the time we give to God becomes the time which God reserves for us in which the Spirit speaks to our spirit" (M. De La Chapelle).

Likewise necessary is the disposition to lend a "religious ear" (Vatican II), to be open to the word of God, which "teaches the truth, bestows charity, and distributes the fruits of wisdom" (Bernard).

These and others like them are the dispositions which create the "good and perfect heart" which "safeguards the Word" until it "produces fruit," as Jesus taught (cf. Lk 8:15). Each one who practices *lectio divina* must act in such a way as to acquire this "heart," as the fruit of one's own effort, but also, and above all, to seek it as a gift of grace. For this reason every *lectio divina* should begin with a prayer: "It is important and absolutely necessary to pray for an understanding of the Scriptures; in fact in them we read that 'it is the Lord who gives wisdom, from Him come all knowledge and understanding' (Pr 2:6)" (Augustine). "To arrive at a mystical understanding of the divine Scriptures and to the science of divine thoughts we will draw more profit from the *oratio* than from profound investigations" (Richard of Saint-Victor).

To this proposition Yussef Busnaya, a Christian writer from Syria, suggests this prayer: "Grant me, O Lord, the words of life and joy from the mouth and tongue of Scripture. Help me to listen with interior ears renewed by the Holy Spirit." Every *lectio divina* will begin, then, with a prayer, above all with an invocation of the Holy Spirit. It is He, in fact, who "disposes the one who reads to be obedient to the word" (Gregory the Great).

## 6. The "holy page": the biblical text

*Lectio divina* refers, by definition, to a *page* (that is to a passage, preferably brief) from Scripture.

Various selections from the "*sacra pagina*," the holy page, are possible. If we want to concentrate on a theme in the *lectio*, we pick a biblical passage on a specific topic: this selection is useful on the occasion of a day of "retreat" (a "desert" day, as they sometimes call it) or of a prolonged time of prayer. If we want to do a continuous or semi-continuous *lectio* of a biblical book, we will likewise pick a passage where the sense is completed. In any case the text should not be too long: a length of between 10 and 20 verses or even less is normally sufficient.

But the holy page around which we might orient ourselves is preferably that proposed by the liturgy for the festivity immediately following (or even preceding) the day in which *lectio divina* is to be practiced. The liturgical approach, in fact, guides us progressively into the mystery of Christ by means of a unified presentation of the Bible and the Christological and Christian interpretation of the Scriptures.

## 7. The "*lectio*": listening

In the practice of *lectio divina* the "time" of the *lectio* is passed in "listening" to the message of the holy page, guided by the interpretation-explanation of the biblical text. We have already shown that the attention in this act of listening focuses more on the concept indicated by the action of "recollection" than it does on that of "reading." *Lectio* is a "reading" of the Scriptures, yes, but the end result, other than that of knowing and understanding the literal sense of the biblical text, lies above all in harvesting the messages, suggestions, and inspirations which are expressed by the sacred text and which we encounter there.

Certainly the *lectio* makes fruitful use of the results of the best in biblical exegesis but, as every exegete knows, one's own interpretation is not equal to nor can it substitute for the divine word. Thus the *lectio* recognizes that its job is not exhausted in the scientific exegesis of the text. The same exegetical research arrives at its proper goal when it is able to make the divine word so persuasive and so involving on the part of the reader as to induce him to offer it the receptivity of his heart and to open himself to what the divine word, always rich in instruction and full of new inspirations, has to say.

It happens in this way that the *lectio* has its confirmation and corroboration in the *auditio*, in the "listening." As it is today, so also in ancient Semitic civilizations, the public reading of a text was done aloud, in such a way as to make listening something natural. But the ancients, even in private, used to read the text pronouncing the words vocally. The text thus assumed a vocal resonance and was perceptible to the ear of the reader.

In such a way memorization took place which was not only mental but also auricular and therefore truly thorough. "The mouth pronounces the words of the text, the memory fixes them in the mind, the intelligence understands their significance, the will desires to translate them into works" (J. Leclercq). "Listening," then, is an openness to the word, capacity to glean its messages, suggestions and inspirations, availability to change what is heard into that which Paul calls the "obedience of faith" (Rm 1:5).

But in the *lectio divina* the eyes, ears and mind constitute for the divine word mere passageways for the *lectio*; its destination, in fact, is the more hidden but truer place of the religious reality of man. The prophet Ezekiel (cf. 3:10) long ago received the order from God to "take into your heart all the words that I speak to you; hear them well." That "heart" is defined by Theophane the Recluse as "the parlor where the Lord is welcomed."

The "time" of the *lectio* is then an important moment in the practice of *lectio divina* in that it leads to an encounter with the divine word. And it is also a sensitive moment because it is here that the specific relationship of each one with the word of God comes into play. Given this importance and this difficulty, in the communitarian practice of *lectio divina* it is appropriate that the *lectio* be led by a person capable of doing so. In any case it will be necessary to take advantage of the interpretations and explanations prepared by scholars. In every language there are commentaries and aids available which answer to the various abilities and characteristics of our Christian communities.

Loving and persevering practice of the *lectio* of the divine word leads day by day into a world filled with marvels, "in the field of the Scripture multicolored flowers, ready for the picking are to be found everywhere. Every species is present there," St. Jerome writes: "red roses, white lilies and flowers of every color: there is an embarrassment of riches. It remains for us but to collect the flowers which seem to us the most beautiful. And if we gather up roses we should not be unhappy that we have not picked lilies; and if we have gathered lilies, we are not disdaining the humble violets." "All is beautiful and fascinating in the sweet land promised to generous souls who have agreed to labor a little among the holy books. They will soon be able and with all wisdom to turn to their Spouse and say to Him: Your words are sweeter than honey to my lips. Nothing is sweeter or better than knowledge of the Scriptures."

## 8. The "*meditatio*": the harvesting

This "time" of the *lectio divina* consists essentially in the theological-spiritual development of the subjects that arise from the *lectio* which Guigo expresses this way: "Meditation considers the interior understanding" of the text. It is an "interior understanding" in that it is an understanding of that which lies beneath the surface of the Scriptures.

According to tradition, *lectio divina* arrives at this by means of practices which are inscribed on the imagination by habitual human actions that derive their impetus from that biblical passage where the prophet is ordered to "eat" the scroll of the word of God (cf. Ezk 3:3; Rv 10:9-10) to signify the almost physical co-penetration that needs to take place between man and the divine word. This image implies the symbol of Scripture as "a sweet and nourishing food" (Augustine), which can be "digested" only after having been chewed (Jerome). From it is derived the image of "mastication" (Gregory the Great) which allows one to "digest" its provisions. Guigo writes: "The *lectio* brings the food to the mouth, the *meditatio* chews it." The symbolism is obvious, but it becomes less so for us today when the medieval authors, applying to it the way in which some animals — cows, for instance — assimilate food, compare the *meditatio* to a *ruminatio*, a "rumination."

All the same, in its metaphorical sense, even in English this term means to reflect at length, to assimilate a message and to contemplate accordingly. In reference to the word of God, *ruminatio* assumes meanings more and more defined by its nuances: to repeat the word that has been heard in a way that it presents itself to the reader in all its concreteness (M.I. Angelini), to return to the meaning of the word in order to enter into the depths of its message, to repeat the word or its essential message in a concise expression so as to be able "to savor" it, to allow the message to descend from the mind which understood it to the "heart," the place which it recognizes as its own proper abode. The profound meaning of *ruminatio* is clarified by St. Caesarius of Arles (6th century) when he explains that it is an "intimate penetration, under the guidance of grace, of the profound wonders of the word of God." The spiritual dimension of *ruminatio* is made explicit by St. Gregory the Great's teaching that it serves to "open the way for the Lord so that He can enter into our hearts and inflame them with the grace of His love."

Even if what is fundamental to *meditatio* remains the property of the individual, all the same, in its communitarian practice, this "time" will also be usefully led by a person who has been adequately prepared. For a good outcome of *lectio divina* it is, in fact, important that the reflection become immediately centered not on marginal considerations, but on subjects which are theologically and spiritually valid.

It is above all in this "time" that the reflections of the Fathers of the Church, masters of the theological-spiritual interpretation of the Bible whose writings cover the whole of the Bible and are often found in English translation, prove fruitful. The *meditatio* derives benefit also from the usefulness of those masters of the spirit of recent times who go under the name of the "new Fathers" of the Church, that is of those theologians who have known how to demonstrate the spiritual constants of the Scriptures, such as R. Guardini, J. Maritain, H.U. von Balthasar, H. de Lubac, Y. Congar, E. Stein, M.-D. Chenu, Elizabeth of the Trinity and many others.

## 9. The *"collatio"*: sharing

Our modern sensibilities reject solipsistic or professorial attitudes in a community, above all if it has come together to reflect and pray. We desire, on the contrary, the personal involvement and appreciate the participation of each one. With regard to *lectio divina* these contemporary requirements find an answer in the teaching that comes from ancient monasticism. In the *Life of St. Antony* (written about 357), St. Athanasius fixed in his memory these words of the holy abbot of the Egyptian desert: "The Sacred Scriptures are enough for teaching, but it would be well if we were at the same time earnestly encouraged in our faith and edified by the words." In the practice of *lectio divina* the deepening of the message of the holy page continues profitably in the *collatio*. With these terms we wish to indicate the input of the participants in the communitarian practice of *lectio divina* for a better appreciation of the message of the word of God and a more incisive actualization of it. Characteristics of the *collatio* are its dialogical character and reciprocal edification in the faith.

In reference to the *meditatio*, the *collatio* recognizes an initial objective in reaching "a greater understanding" of the word of God. St. Isidore of Seville (6th century), among the many aphorisms of the early Fathers which he copied, has handed also this one down to us: "The *collatio* is better than the *lectio*. In fact, if the *lectio*, useful for learning, is accompanied by the *collatio*, a greater understanding is obtained" of the sacred text. "By comparing ideas, what at first seemed obscure or doubtful becomes clear."

This text of St. Isidore is taken up and commented on by M. Magrassi: "Isidore begins by affirming the superiority of the *collatio* over individual reading. He then describes the fundamental attitude by which this *collatio* ought to be animated: a receptive availability towards others. Summing up the lights and experiences that are granted to each one, we go more deeply into our understanding of the word. The questions, the responses and the objections stimulate a more lively research; all, thus, becomes clearer."

Regarding the content and the style of the *collatio*, a discourse on three Latin terms rich in meaning which has come down to us from the pen of the medieval Benedictine monk Smaragdus is enlightening. The *collatio* is a "*collocutio*" (=a culturally binding dialogue), a "*confabulatio*" (=a fraternal conversation), and a "*confessio*" (=bringing of a personal testimony). It often happens that the practice of the *collatio* leads to the constitution of a community of faith.

Some advice of a practical nature will be useful. By its very nature the *collatio* is a group dialogue, a communitarian conversation, and as such requires the participation of several persons. The willingness to learn is the spirit with which one must participate. If the *collatio* were to degenerate into a dispute, its purpose — that of being the contribution by many voices to a common edification in the faith, a growth in charity and a comfort in hope — would be derailed. The same communitarian *lectio divina* would end by losing its very identity: in it, in fact, brothers of faith come together to be taught by the divine word and to support one another in the arduous task of building in and around themselves the Kingdom of God. Each one ought therefore to be on their guard and the one who presides over the communitarian *lectio divina* must gently see to it that the *collatio* does not become (even involuntarily) led into paths of discussion which are vaguely social or political or anthropological or at least generically cultural.

Although exposed to some risks, all the same the *collatio* is something very positive which M. Olphe-Galliard sums up in this way: "The *collatio* has to nourish itself on Sacred Scripture and reflect a personal experience of the interior life. It doesn't require flights of erudition even if at the same time simple outbursts of devotion are not sufficient." "Today we are taking part in a rebirth of interest in the *collatio*; this is explained by the need which Christians have of feeling united in a spiritual community." The risks "of vain discourse, of childishness and of sentimentalism" will be avoided by the deliberation and rigorous reference to the teachings which come from the *lectio* and the *meditatio*.

## 10. The *"oratio"*: prayer

By its very nature prayer is something exquisitely personal, an expression of the reality of our relationship with God. For that reason each one will live this "time" of *lectio divina* in a way which allows them to better enter into dialogue and communion with God.

From the religiosity of the pagans we Christians have learned all too well how to multiply prayers, above all, those of petition. Monasticism, in *lectio divina* has kept and re-proposes even in our own day prayer as the word of God, "read, meditated on and spoken back" to God. In such a way the preoccupation of thinking up formulas for our prayer is taken away. When "the word of God ascends, like incense, without a sound and gently to heaven" (E. Bianchi), it is already prayer, and authentic prayer at that.

The *oratio*, then, flows spontaneously from

the encounter of the "heart" of man "with the heart of God by means of the word of God" (Gregory the Great). In such a way, as for the *meditatio*, we are brought back to the "heart" which — according to the purest biblical and spiritual tradition — "is the most intimate part of man, the place where God dwells" (Theophane the Recluse). In it that encounter in which God speaks to man and man listens to God takes place; man speaks to God and God listens to man: all through the one divine Word. Smaragdus affirms that prayer "is the work of the heart, not of the lips, because God pays attention not to the words but to the heart of the one who prays." While approaching from his own particular point of view, F. Fénelon (1651-1715) wisely wrote: "True prayer is that of the heart."

The way to the finish line of the authenticity of prayer is, therefore, love, which "is by its nature communion." And thus true prayer is the thrust towards God known by love and a dialogue in the sign of love, which has no need of words to express itself. It is in reference also to this that Jesus cautioned: "When you pray, do not multiply words" (cf. Mt 6:7).

It can happen, however, that for various reasons "you are overcome by the blessed desire to say something." In this case the masters of prayer, both ancient and modern, teach us to do this: "Choose a word, a short phrase which well expresses your love for God, and then repeat it, repeat it with peace, without seeking to formulate any thoughts." Pray, that is, according to the model — today much sought after — which has come to be called "the prayer of the heart."

In the communitarian practice of *lectio divina* it might be useful to the common edification of the group to compose some expressions of prayer. The responsibility that each one has towards the other participants requires vigilance so that "it does not happen that our prayer comes from earth rather than from heaven." "From earth comes prayer which is spiritual chatter." The prayer "born of earth, remains on earth, rich only in its own uselessness."

From heaven, instead, comes the prayer which flows to us from the word of God which has been given to us to know in the *lectio* and in the *meditatio* and which rises up in us through the grace of the "Spirit, which comes to our aid in our weakness" (Rm 8:26). It is the Spirit which stirs up in us true prayer: "To us is left the job of repeating what the Spirit suggests to us and gives us the power to utter" (C. Carretto).

To assist in the undoubted difficulty to pray in this way, it is useful to have recourse to texts drawn from the liturgy or from the writings of the saints, even if the best form remains that of reiterating what was grasped from the *lectio* and the *meditatio* on the word of God.

## 11. The *"contemplatio"*: communion

It is impossible to express in general terms what *contemplatio* is insofar as it is a very highly personal experience of God. The masters of the spirit describe it this way: "prayer of silence," "prayer of repose," "prayer of the presence of God," "prayer of pure faith," "prayer of the heart alone."

F. Fénelon (17th century) teaches how to live it: "Desire your Beloved Spouse." "Desire is love." "And love is insatiable for love."

For the scope of concretely recognizing *contemplatio* a text from the mystic John of Fécamp (ca. 990-1078) may be of some help. He felt he had to express it in the form of a prayer: "My spirit raises up to you, only God, a heart that is pure. Everything is still, all is calm, my heart burns with love. My soul overflows with joy, my memory with vigor, my understanding with light. And my whole spirit, inflamed with the desire to see your beauty, feels itself enraptured by love of invisible realities." In a certain measure *contemplatio* puts us in touch with "the hidden face of God" (William of Saint-Thierry) and then "the soul rests in joy and repose because it possesses the One it loves" (St. Thomas Aquinas). St. Bernard adds great realism to contemplation, writing that it "catches God and almost touches Him." "You touch Him with the hand of faith, with the embrace of devotion, with the eyes of the mind." Impressed by the realism of his own expression, St. Bernard almost corrects himself: "You touch God not with the hand but with love, not with the senses but with faith." And he concludes: "To believe is to see."

The "time" of the *contemplatio* does not necessarily have a specific place in the plan for the development of *lectio divina* insofar as it can exist in the same way that it is lived. If, however, one wants to find a place for *contemplatio* in the scheme of things, then it could find a place after the *meditatio* and in this case bring to fruition the theological truths considered, or else after the *oratio* and then it would constitute its follow-up and highest expression. Obviously it is a "time" to be lived in an absolutely personal way.

Masters of the spirit teach that "one must never give precedence to contemplation over meditation." In fact meditation is always possible;

contemplation, no, because it is a gift of divine grace. And so "if contemplation is lacking, it is necessary to take up meditation once again, as the sailor uses the oars when the wind no longer fills the sails" (Fénelon).

Notwithstanding its difficulty, precisely for the fact that it is the summit of knowledge and love, *contemplatio* constitutes "one of the essential elements of the Christian life" and hence it "should exist in every Christian." It may be in him only in a "germinal state, but it is hoped that this germ will develop in the greatest possible measure, in proportion to the generosity and charity of each one" (St. Isidore of Seville).

## 12. The *"operatio"*: witness

Only those who are superficial pragmatists can imagine an *operatio* apart from *contemplatio*. *Operatio* is the putting into practice of the fruits of *contemplatio* and *meditatio* as well. The influence of *lectio divina* on *operatio* must be global, total. It is not a matter of extrapolating from Scripture a maxim to use as an operative objective: this would be a fleeting and superficial solution. Nor is it a matter of validating with a biblical maxim a line of action already chosen: the

Bible is not a series of maxims to put into practice. On the contrary, it is a matter of allowing the word to flow into me and us who have come together for *lectio divina*, allowing the word to be — as we embrace it — the source of enlightenment, proposals and working projects, making us, yes, ready for "obedience."

It is not we who propose projects to God nor ought we to ask Him to confirm with His word projects planned by us. The word of God is given to us as that which opens up horizons and teaches the ways in which they can be reached. According to St. Paul everything comes from God: it is He in fact who stirs up in us both "to desire" and "to work"; it is up to us to meet the demands of "His good purposes" because only these fulfill the plan of God (cf. Ph 2:13).

The indications that come from *lectio divina* in reference to the *operatio* can seem more or less general to some. Instead nothing is so concrete and efficacious as giving ear to the Word of God who shares the reality of the living God: "All things came to be through Him, and without Him nothing came to be" (Jn 1:3). So it is the Word who originates every true project of the *operatio* and it is the grace of the Spirit which gives success to every undertaking of the *operatio*.

The medieval mystical theologian Hugh of

Saint-Victor notes that there exist "many persons who, being deprived of discernment" don't allow the *meditatio* and the *contemplatio* to inspire and vivify their activity. Thus "they work very hard but obtain scarce results."

These wise observations of Hugh introduce us to the essential problems of *operatio* following on *lectio divina. Operatio,* in fact, is not related to the word of God as if the word of God might serve to confirm operational choices and chosen conduct in another setting. On the contrary, the selection of the duties of the *operatio* and the means of realizing them flow spontaneously from listening to the divine word, which often can seem not to indicate with too much detail what one is to do in the reality of one's situation. In truth, the word of God always goes to the essence of things and of our being, and only teaches what is essentially valid. About this and around it multiple and diverse operative choices are possible, responding to diverse situations, but always enlightened by the divine word.

# Conclusion

In conclusion, a proposal to wrap things up and a piece of advice.

*Lectio divina* can be broadly described in these terms: God is listened to in the *lectio*, His words are taken to heart in the *meditatio*, they edify the community of faith in the *collatio*, they are changed into our words to Him in the *oratio*, become communion with Him and with the mystery of His love in the *contemplatio*, and they lead us to action in the *operatio* as a discovery of our responsibilities in life in the light and grace of the Spirit.

*Lectio divina* is lived in a tranquil state of soul, in serenity and peace, because it allows for a generous opening up to the message of the word and prompt availability to the suggestions of the Spirit. From the development of *lectio divina* all forms of rigidity, constraint, and force must be banned. *Lectio divina* is a walk toward God, and for that reason, as in any walk, so in this, everything has to be proportioned to the pace, the strength, the rhythm of those who are walking. The result toward which we tend is not the realization of some plan of growth and development, but the free and gentle utilization of *lectio divina* in the service of achieving an encounter with God through His word, listened to, taken to heart, shared, prayed over, contemplated, assimilated and lived in everyday life.

# Bibliography

à Kempis, Thomas. *The Imitation of Christ*, Alba House, Staten Island, NY, 1982, 1992, 1997.

Angelini, M.I. *Il monaco e la parabola. Saggio sulla spiritualità monastica della lectio divina*, Morcelliana, Brescia, 1981.

Bianchi, E. *Pregare la Parola. Introduzione alla "lectio divina"* (La parola di Dio, 10), Gribaudi, Torino, 1980.

Bloom, Anthony. *Beginning to Pray*, Paulist Press, Mahwah, NJ, 1982.

_____. *Courage to Pray*, St. Vladimirs, 1984.

Bovenmars, Jan G. *A Biblical Spirituality of the Heart*, Alba House, Staten Island, NY, 1991.

Catoir, John T. *Enjoy the Lord*, Alba House, Staten Island, NY, 1988.

de la Potterie, I. *The Hour of Jesus*, Alba House, Staten Island, NY, 1990.

Gaudoin-Parker, Michael L. *Heart in Pilgrimage*, Alba House, Staten Island, NY, 1994.

_____. *The Real Presence Through the Ages*, Alba House, Staten Island, NY, 1993.

_____. *A Window on the Mystery of Faith*, Alba House, Staten Island, NY, 1997.

Giudici, M.P. *Lectio divina e communità-communione,* in "Consacrazione e servizio," 35 (1986), n. 6, pp. 19-23; nn. 7-8, pp. 18-23.

Guigo II il Certosino. *La scala di Giacobbe,* in *Tornerò al mio cuore,* ed. Qiqajon, Bose 1987, pp. 27-41. Text also in *Lettera ai Certosini,* a cura di A. Scaglione Pomilio, Rusconi, Milano 1983, pp. 133-153; in Aa.vv. *Un itinerario di contemplazione,* Edizioni Paoline, Cinisello Balsamo, 1987, pp. 21-34.

Harrington, Wilfrid. *Key to the Bible* (3 vols.), Alba House, Staten Island, NY, 1975.

_____. *The Rosary: A Gospel Prayer,* Alba House, Staten Island, NY, 1975.

Kaitholil, G. *The Prayer Called Life,* St. Pauls, Homebush, NSW, 1991.

Lawrence, Brother. *Practice of the Presence of God,* Alba House, Staten Island, NY, 1997.

Leclercq, J. *Lectio divina,* in DIP, vol. V, Roma 1978, pp. 561-566.

Magrassi, M. *Bibbia e preghiera. La lectio divina,* Ancora, Milano 1990.[8]

_____. *Pregare la Bibbia,* in Aa.vv., *Incontro con la Bibbia* (Biblioteca di scienze religiose, 23), Las, Roma 1978, pp. 121-130.

_____. *Vivere la Parola,* ed. La scala, Noci 1979.

Martini, C.M. *Journeying with the Lord,* Alba House, Staten Island, NY, 1987.

Masini, M. *Iniziazione alla lectio divina. Teologia, metodo, spiritualità, prassi* (Ascolta la Parola), ed. Messaggero, Padova 1996.[4]

_____. *La lectio divina. Teologia, spiritualità, metodo* (Parola di Dio, 2ª serie, 15), San Paolo, Milano 1996.

Oury, G.-M. *Cercare Dio nella sua Parola. La lectio divina* (Parola e liturgia, 17), Paoline 1986.

Pinckaers, Servais. *The Pursuit of Happiness — God's Way*, Alba House, Staten Island, NY, 1998.

Taylor, Michael. *Paul: His Letters, Message and Heritage*, Alba House, Staten Island, NY, 1997.

Torkington, David. *Inner Life: A Fellow Traveller's Guide to Prayer* with Foreword by Sister Wendy Beckett, Alba House, Staten Island, NY, 1998.

Vagaggini, C. and Penco, G. (a cura di), *La preghiera nella Bibbia e nella tradizione patristica e monastica* (Biblioteca di cultura religiosa, 2ª s., 78), Paoline, Roma 1964.